INTO YOUR HANDS

Michael T. Winstanley SDB

INTO YOUR HANDS

Gospel reflections

ST PAULS

INTO YOUR HANDS: Gospel reflections
©Michael T. Winstanley SDB, 1993

First published, April 1994

National Library of Australia
Cataloguing-in-Publication data:
Winstanley, Michael T.
Into your hands: gospel reflections
ISBN 1 875570 28 4
1. Bible. N.T. Gospels — Criticism, interpretation, etc. 2 Trust in God — Christianity.
3. Christian life — Biblical teaching. 4. Image of God — Biblical teaching. I. Title.
(Series: Biblical studies; 3).
226.06

Cover photo: Lores Riva, © Periodici San Paolo, Milan, Italy.
Christ, 6th century mosaic, Basilica of the Assumption, Venice.
Cover design: Bruno Colombari SSP

Imprimi Potest: Michael Cunningham SDB
            Provincial of Salesians of Don Bosco, Britain

Published by
ST PAULS — Society of St Paul,
60-70 Broughton Road — (PO Box 230) — Homebush, NSW 2140

ST PAULS is an activity of the Priests and Brothers of the Society of St Paul who proclaim the Gospel through the media of social communication.

For
Ruth and Frank and Martin
and in memory of
Fr H. Wrangham SDB

ACKNOWLEDGEMENTS

Extracts taken from:

New English Bible ©1970, used by permission of Oxford and Cambridge University Presses, UK.

Revised English Bible ©1989, used by permission of Oxford and Cambridge University Presses, UK.

The *Jerusalem Bible*, published and copyright 1966, 1967 and 1968 by Darton, Longman and Todd Ltd and Doubleday & Co. Inc., and used by permission of the publishers.

The *New Jerusalem Bible*, published and copyright 1985 by Darton, Longman and Todd Ltd and Doubleday & Co. Inc., and used by permission of the publishers.

Come and See, Michael Winstanley, published and copyright 1985 by Darton, Longman and Todd Ltd and used by permission of the publishers.

The Gospel According to St Mark, M.D. Hooker, 1991, London, A. & C. Black.

The Good News According to Mark, E. Schweizer, 1971, London, SPCK.

Mark, Wilfrid Harrington, 1979, Dublin, Veritas.

The Gospel According to St John, R. Schnackenburg, 1968, London, Burns & Oates.

The Gospel According to St John, C.K. Barrett, 1978, London, SPCK.

The Gospel According to John R.E. Brown, 1972, London, Cassell.

The Gospel According to Luke (vol. 1 1981; vol. 2 1985), J.A. Fitzmyer, New York, Doubleday.

The Pelican New Testament Commentaries: The Gospel of St Luke, © G.B. Caird, 1963, London, Penguin.

The Sayings of Jesus, T.W. Manson, 1971, London, SCM.

The Hour of Jesus, I. de la Potterie, 1989, Slough, St Paul.

Jesus and Woman, F.J. Moloney, in F. Bergamelli and M. Cimosa (eds), *Virgo Fidelis, Studi Mariani*, 1988, Rome, Edizioni Liturgiche.

Mary in the Mystery of the Covenant, I. de la Potterie, 1992, New York, Alba.

In Memory of Her: a feminist theological reconstruction of Christian origins, Elisabeth Schussler Fiorenza, © 1983, New York, Crossroad.

Inside Christian Community, R. Hammett & L. Sofield, 1982, Hartford, Jesuit Educational Center for Human Development.

Spiritual Friendship, Aelred of Rievulx (ed. A. Squire), 1977, Kalamazoo, Cistercian.

Intimacy and the Hungers of the Heart, P. Collins, 1991, Dublin, Columba.

Poet and Peasant and Through Peasants' Eyes (combined edition), K.E. Bailey, 1983, Grand Rapids, Eerdmans.

Poets, Prophets, Pragmatists, © Evelyn Woodward, 1987, Melbourne, Collins Dove.

Honest to God, J.A.T. Robinson, 1963, London, SCM.

The Shepherd Image in the Scriptures: a Paradigm for Christian Ministry, in *The Clergy Review*, Vol. LXXI, no. 6, 1986, Cambridge, Blackfriars.

Revised chapter (Celebrating at Cana), in *Religious Life Review*, vol. 31, July/August 1992, W.T. Winstanley, Dublin, Dominican.

Christ the Sacrament, E. Schillebeeckx, 1963, London, Sheed & Ward.

All used by permission of the publishers.

CONTENTS

INTRODUCTION

For all those striving to live as Christian disciples, the word of God in scripture is a source of enlightenment and inspiration. In my own efforts I have found the insights of biblical scholars, as they grapple with shape and meaning, enriching for both mind and heart. I am obliged to admit, however, that the complexities and technicalities of modern scholarship can at times be bewildering, and that many Christians consequently become discouraged from exploring further.

This book is an attempt to bridge the gap, and to share the results of contemporary biblical research with a wider audience, in the conviction that thereby our understanding and prayer will be deepened, and the quality of our discipleship enhanced.

The topics developed in the pages which follow are themes which I have found particularly interesting and stimulating personally, and which I have reflected upon with others in pastoral and prayer contexts. They have been rethought and revised during a few months' break kindly offered to me after I had finished my term of ministry as Provincial of the Salesians of Don Bosco in Britain.

There are two threads which link the topics together. The first is the desire to 'be with' Jesus (which is Mark's manner of describing discipleship in 3:14), in some of the key situations of his life. In this way we can visit some of the important places and encounter some of the main personalities in his story. We shall share the Matthaean Christmas experience, the Cana wedding celebration, Jesus' encounters with the 'little people', and his table companionship. We shall spend time in Jerusalem and at Calvary, and we shall also explore some of the imagery, which his environment, and the history of his people, suggested to him.

As I made this 'journey' in preparing the material for publication, and sought to sew the topics together, another thread gradually emerged, the motif of trust. This theme has two closely correlated aspects. I became increasingly aware of the image of God revealed in Jesus: a God of providential care, compassion and forgiveness; a God who comes in search of us, and offers us friendship and life; a God who is manifestly worthy of our trust. At the same time, I realised that the response sought for in the various situations, and given in so many different ways, could be described as trust. And one day the title suggested itself: *Into Your Hands*.

'Father, into your hands I commit my spirit' is the prayer which Luke places on the lips of the dying Jesus (23:46). It is taken from Psalm 31, which is the prayer of one in great distress, surrounded by enemies, who takes refuge in the Lord, and puts hope and confidence in the faithful love of Yahweh, in God's saving vindication. These words epitomise Jesus' trust and his surrender to the God whom he knows and addresses characteristically as 'Abba', a term which seems to have captured his understanding and intimate experience of God. His prayer is a statement of faith in the God-who-raises-from-the-dead, who 'will not abandon me to death, nor let your faithful servant suffer corruption' (Ps 16:10 in Acts 2:27).

It is my hope that this book will help us to come to know the God of Jesus more closely, and to grow in the trusting surrender of our lives into God's gracious hands.

In the reflections I have drawn considerably on the work of many scripture scholars. To these I here express my gratitude. In the Notes I have attempted to acknowledge the authors on whom I have depended. The biblical quotations are taken mainly from *The Revised English Bible*, the revisers of which 'have preferred more inclusive gender reference where that has been possible without compromising scholarly integrity or English style'. Further progress remains to be made, however, in this rightly sensitive area, and I apologise for any offence which may be caused.

I wish to thank Fr Julian Fox, who kindly invited me to spend my sabbatical in Melbourne, and the members of the Salesian Community of Oakleigh for their generous hospitality and friendship. I owe a large debt of gratitude to Fr Frank Moloney, a long-standing friend, who shared with me the fruits of his scholarship and his love for God's word, and offered me encouragement, criticism, useful suggestions, and access to his library, thus rendering possible the completion of this project. Thanks also to Ruth and Kieran for reading the manuscript and helping me to clarify thought and expression, and to all involved

in its final publication. Finally, I would like to thank the
many disciples of Jesus, whose support, example and
friendship have enriched and sustained me through the
years.

Michael T. Winstanley, SDB

1 | STARGAZING

It is unfortunate that we are exposed to the fascination and challenge of the second chapter of Matthew's Gospel only at Christmastide, and that during this liturgical period it tends to be eclipsed by the Lukan version of the events surrounding the birth of Jesus. It is no less unfortunate that folkloristic elements are apt to grasp our imagination, and historical considerations distract our attention, so that the theological significance of the narrative, valid for every day and season, sinks into the shadows. In this opening chapter, I would like to reflect with you on three aspects of the Matthaean narrative which I believe can touch our lives today as individuals and as church community.[1]

---

1   Readers familiar with R.E. Brown's *The Birth of the Messiah* (London, Chapman 1978), will recognise my indebtedness to his scholarship. Other books which have proved helpful include: F.W. Beare, *The Gospl according to Matthew* (Oxford, Blackwell 1981); W.D. Davies and D.C. Allison, *A Critical and Exegetical Commentary on the Gospel according to Saint Matthew*

JOURNEYING UNDER THE GAZE OF GOD

In the first place we are confronted with a chapter of journeying – a topical and relevant motif for most of us. The whole chapter is, in fact, dominated by geographical names and journeys. There is the journey of the Magi from their home in the exotic East (be that Arabia or Babylon, Parthia or Syria), the seat of astrology and religious wisdom, to Jerusalem and on to Bethlehem, David's ancestral town, and away again (Mt 2:1-12). Later there is the journey of the Holy Family from Bethlehem to Egypt and back to the land of Israel, the region of Galilee and the town of Nazareth (Mt 2:13-23). As the role of the angelic messengers, the dreams, and the scriptural quotations indicate, these journeys are undertaken at God's instigation and are completed beneath God's providential gaze. The Lord is with the travellers 'in their coming and their going', as the Celtic prayer phrases it, echoing Psalm 121:8.

1. The journeys of the Holy Family

In the mind of the evangelist, these family journeys evoke other journeys in the experience of the people of Israel: the descent into Egypt in the time of the first Joseph, the return under Moses, and the re-entry into the Promised Land under Joshua, whose name, like that of Jesus, means 'Yahweh saves'. The narrative has a strikingly close parallel

(I.C.C., Edinburgh, T & T Clark 1988); H.B. Green, *The Gospel according to Matthew* (Oxford, Clarendon 1975); U. Luz, *Matthew 1-7, A Commentary* (Edinburgh, T & T Clark 1990); J.P. Meier, *Matthew* (Dublin, Veritas 1980); F.J. Moloney, *Beginning the Good News* (Sydney, St Paul Publications 1992).

in the story of Moses, whose life was threatened by Pharaoh's decree that all Hebrew male children should be killed (Ex 1:22), and who escaped the threat of death by being rescued from the waters of the Nile (cf. Ex 2:1-9). Again, later in life, after murdering the Egyptian who had been maltreating one of the Hebrew workers, he was forced to escape Pharaoh's hostility by going into exile in Midian (Ex 2:15). On the death of Pharaoh (Ex 4:19) Yahweh ordered him to return to his people and save them from slavery, liberating them in the Exodus event. God was clearly with him in his coming and his going.

Jesus relives the experience of Moses, the first redeemer and liberator, founder of the covenanted People of God. In Matthew's eyes, Jesus is the new Moses, transposing the mosaic role and functions on to a higher plane, into a totally new dimension.

The journey into Egypt, and the return, reflect the early Christian intuition that the history of ancient Israel was the preparation for Jesus' career. The infant Jesus is reliving the history of his people. Jesus is the new Israel. To underline this, Matthew uses explicit scriptural quotations with great art and considerable originality and freedom.[2]

---

2   These formula quotations indicate the conviction that the New Testament is the fulfilment of the Old. It was a way of proving that God had foretold Jesus' career, and that everything, even minor details, was part of God's plan. This would give support to the faith of Christian readers, particularly in the situation after the break of the Christian community with Israel. It would have both an apologetic and didactic value. It was the way in which the Christian community laid claim to the bible. The quotations also emphasise Matthew's theological and pastoral insights and themes, particularly his christological standpoint. See U. Luz, *Matthew*, pp. 156-164; R.E. Brown, *Birth*, pp. 184-187.

After stating that Joseph took the child and mother to Egypt, he concludes this stage of the narrative by asserting:

> This was to fulfil what the Lord had declared through the prophet: 'Out of Egypt I have called my son' (Mt 2:15).

He is citing Hosea 11:1 ('When Israel was a youth I loved him; out of Egypt I called my son'), applying directly to Jesus a verse which unambiguously refers to Israel, and also claiming explicitly that Jesus is God's Son. He develops this conviction in the next two chapters, in his presentation of Jesus' baptism and temptations.

This typological equation of Jesus with Israel is similarly found in the quotation from Jeremiah in connection with the massacre of the Bethlehem children (Mt 2:18). Jeremiah 31 is, in fact, a chapter of hope, depicting the happy day on which the exiles will return to the land of Israel. Matthew sees these words, originally spoken to Israel, as equally applicable to Israel's messiah.[3] He associates the weeping of Rachel, the ancestral mother of Israel, with Ramah, near Bethlehem, the place of her burial according to one tradition (Gen 35:16-20; 48:7). It was at Ramah that the captives from Jerusalem and Judaea gathered for their journey into Babylonian exile. Thus the evangelist links the departure of Jesus to Egypt, amidst the grief associated with the massacre of the children, with the lamentation accompanying the depar-

---

3   See W.D. Davies and D.C. Allison, *Saint Matthew*, p. 267. Rachel was buried north of Jerusalem near Bethel in the territory of Benjamin on the way to Ephratha (1 Sam 10:2). Jeremiah implies this, as Rachel's voice is heard in Ramah, halfway between Jerusalem and Bethel. There was an alternative site near Bethlehem, south of Jerusalem, probably due to the settling there of some of the clan of Ephrath. The confusion was convenient for Matthew!

ture of Israel into exile, and with the hope of a return. He links him with the two nadir moments of Israel's history: the persecution in Egypt and the exile in Babylon. From both, the Lord eventually delivered the people. Jesus, then, relives this experience of exodus, exile and return; he is the new Israel.

The journey motif and the infancy narrative terminate with the arrival of the Holy Family in Nazareth, an insignificant agricultural village of Galilee, which had no messianic pretensions and is never mentioned in the Old Testament.

> This was to fulfil the words spoken through the prophets: 'He shall be called a Nazarene' (Mt 2:23).

It is difficult to identify the source of this saying. There is probably an allusion to the *nazir*, the holy man consecrated to God from the womb like Samson and Samuel (cf. Judg 13:2-7; 16:17; Num 6:1-21; Is 4:3). There is also a reference to the messianic branch (*neser*) from the root of Jesse (Is 11:1; cf. also 4:2-3).

The term encapsulates Matthew's conviction concerning the person and mission of Jesus. He is indeed the Holy One of God (cf. Mk 1:24), and the Davidic messiah, and he is the man from Nazareth, from Galilee of the Gentiles, beyond the Jordan, where:

> The people that have lived in darkness have seen a great light; light has dawned on those who lived in the land of death's dark shadow (Mt 4:12-17).

It was the plan of God that from that part of Palestine, he would move out to inaugurate his proclamation of the good news.

2. The journeys of the Magi

The Magi's journey, with which our narrative commences, is undertaken in response to a heavenly sign, a revelation in nature. As astrologers and sages, they associate the rising of the star with the birth of a new king; they recognise the signs of the times. It is thought that Isaiah 60:1-6 and Psalm 72:10-11 lie behind the story:

> Arise, shine, Jerusalem, for your light has come,
> and over you the glory of the Lord has dawned.
> Though darkness covers the earth
> and dark night the nations,
> on you the Lord shines
> and over you his glory will appear;
> nations will journey towards your light
> and kings to your radiance...
> ... Camels in droves will cover the land,
> young camels from Midian and Ephah,
> all coming from Sheba
> laden with gold and frankincense,
> heralds of the Lord's praise.
>
> May the kings of Tarshish and of the isles bring gifts,
> the kings of Sheba and Seba present their tribute.
> Let all kings pay him homage,
> all nations serve him.

The evangelist sees the arrival of these Gentiles in search of the new-born king as the fulfilment of God's promises. Their coming illustrates the claim made in the genealogy with which the Gospel begins (Mt 1:1), that Jesus is the son of Abraham, in whom all the nations of the world would be blessed (Gen 22:18). The timing and route of their departure homewards is communicated by God in a dream, and they obey without question. God is with them in their coming and their going.

Central to the Magi story is the response given to their innocent, but profoundly provocative question, concerning the whereabouts of 'the newborn king of the Jews'. The religious élite, summoned by Herod, and asked about the birthplace of 'the Christ', unhesitatingly provide the answer:

> At Bethlehem in Judaea, for this is what the prophet wrote: 'And you, Bethlehem, in the land of Judah, you are by no means the least among the rulers of Judah; for from you will come a ruler to be shepherd of my people Israel' (Mt 2:5-6).

The quotation, which is not introduced by the usual fulfilment formula, is a conflation of Micah 5:1, 2 Samuel 5:2, and 1 Chronicles 11:2, with some adjustment. Again, the identity and role of Jesus are emphasised. He is born in the city of David, the shepherd king. He is the son of David (as asserted in the genealogy), the awaited messiah, the king of the Jews, and his mission is to be shepherd of his people. In passing, it is perhaps worth noting that Moses, too, was thought of as a shepherd (Is 63:11).

Matthew's narrative is a tapestry thickly woven with scriptural threads, a tapestry which illustrates compellingly God's providential presence throughout the history of the people of God in all their coming and their going, in their highs and in their lows, and God's close presence in the dawning story of Jesus of Nazareth.

The journeys provide a framework within which the evangelist expresses and proclaims his understanding of the person and mission of Jesus. It is evident that the significant details of the early life of Jesus, including even the terrible events, fulfil the promises and saving plan of God.

Matthew's narrative is an invitation to us to deepen our trust in the faithful, saving love of God, made present in our world in the person of Jesus, Emmanuel, God-with-us. It is also an invitation to trace God's providential presence in the twisting and turning, the ups and downs of our own life journey, *our* coming and going.

For the Matthaean Jesus assures his disciples that he is with us always, to the end of time (Mt 28:20). In this era of planning, insurances, qualifications and technological wizardry, this age of the 'instant', it has become more difficult, perhaps, to maintain an awareness of God's providence in our personal and community lives.

ON STAR-GAZING

The story of the star and of the wise men coming from the east in search of a king would not have seemed unusual to the people of Matthew's time.[4] Nor was it uncommon to associate astronomical phenomena with the birth or death of royalty. There was widespread popular belief that each person had his or her star, a bright one for the wealthy and important, a dim one for the poor and insignificant. There is also Old Testament background to the story. In Numbers 22-24 a kind of magus, Balaam, was prevailed upon by the evil king Balak to speak in condemnation of Israel. However, under the inspiration of God, he uttered a prophecy that 'a star will come forth out of Israel' (24:17 The Septuagint), 'he will rule many nations' (24:7). In time this oracle came to have messianic meaning.[5]

4   See W.D. Davies and D.C. Allison, *Saint Matthew*, pp. 230-231 and 233-234.
5   See F.J. Moloney, *Beginning the Good News*, p. 91.

One of the Aramaic Targums, which reflect current biblical interpretation in synagogue worship, reads:

> I see him but not now; I behold him but not nigh. When a king shall arise out of Jacob, and the messiah be anointed from Israel, he will slay the princes of Moab and reign over all the children of men.

Perhaps Matthew considered the Magi as Balaam's successors, witnessing the fulfilment of his prophecy, just as they fulfil the prophecy of Isaiah referred to earlier, inaugurating the pilgrimage of the nations to Jerusalem.

After their encounter with Herod in Jerusalem, the star reappears and leads them to the house where the child and his mother are to be found (cf. Ex 4:20). There, with great joy, they prostrate themselves in worship, in recognition of the presence and majesty of God. Such worship marks the culmination of their quest and the climax of this stage of the narrative. They offer their precious gifts as an expression of their loyalty and submission, gifts of myrrh, and of gold and incense, as Isaiah had foretold (Is 60:6).

The image of the star is profoundly symbolic. I like to think of it in two ways. The star is a beckoning star. It has something to do with my call to become really me, with the journey into truth and integrity, the ongoing attempt to be true to what is deepest within me and to fulfil that potential.

God, I believe, calls me by name at the centre of my being. It is there that I am most alone before God in my utter uniqueness. The journey entails risk; it can be lonely at times and confused, giving rise to much self-questioning and the struggle with uncertainty, anxiety and fear. Sometimes it may create painful misunderstanding, conflict even. Still, the star exerts an irresistible attraction and pull; and it leads in the direction of greater freedom, wholeness, and life. It invites me to trusting surrender to God's immense love and faithfulness, and to experience that God is with me in my coming and my going.

Secondly, I believe that there can be many stars in my life. The star is a symbol of God's breaking into my life time and time again, beckoning me forward into the unfolding of God's saving mystery.

Often my awareness is dull, and I fail to notice the star. At times I just do not want to see any star; I prefer cloudy nights. There are occasions when I am aware of its rising, but I choose to ignore it; I do not allow it to impinge, to disturb my routine, to dislodge me from my rut, to attract me into something new — new ideas, new vision, new dimensions of living and of outreach.

I recoil from the risk of moving forward, moving out and away, leaving what is familiar and safe, journeying into uncharted territory. Courage and trust and surrender do not come easily; but the stars continue to beckon.

A correlative facet of star-gazing is my reaction and response to other star-gazers. They can often be uncomfortable folk with whom to live and work. Their seeing can trigger areas of anxiety and fear within me, or can stimulate fresh vision and questions and perspectives.

I am called not only to tolerate them, but also to accept, encourage and support them in their quest to follow their star, to offer help in discerning perhaps, to create spaces for freedom, and to become a more empathetic travelling companion.

RESPONSE TO THE CHILD

One of the major theological themes in this chapter of Matthew is that of response. As well as looking backwards and recapitulating the history of Israel, the narrative looks forward and offers a kind of preview of the ministry of Jesus, in which he will be accepted by some, but rejected and done to death by the Jewish religious leaders and the secular power. Killed in Jerusalem, the centre of opposition, he will reappear in Galilee, Galilee of the Gentiles, as the risen one, the messiah, and receive the worship of his disciples, whom he will send to all nations. It is also a preview of the history of the Church until the time of Matthew's writing.

The good news that Jesus is Messiah and Son of God was preached to the Jews first: some believed and offered him their loyal submission, whereas others refused to accept him. The Pharisees in general, despite their knowledge of the scriptures, were hostile to Christian claims. The Gentiles, however, were turning in faith to Christ in increasing numbers.

The infancy narrative can also present us with a preview of *our* response to the perennial challenge of the coming of Jesus, a response which is probably far from consistent. In the dénouement of the plot, two alternatives are highlighted and dramatically contrasted.

1. The positive response

The positive response is focused firstly in the Magi, who are open to the God who breaks into their lives, and who leave the security of their homeland to take the risk of following their star. A particularly significant aspect of their identity for the evangelist, as we have seen, lies in their being Gentiles. Jesus is the son of Abraham (Mt 1:1) in whom all nations of the world are to be blessed; and we are heirs to that blessing.

We, Gentiles as we are, have been invited to search for the Lord, have been called into the circle of God's love and life. The writer of the letter to the Ephesians expresses with remarkable force and clarity this mystery of God's generous and open love extended also to us (Eph 2:11-22). It is a gift to which we should strive not to grow too accustomed, a gift not to be taken for granted, a gift to grasp repeatedly in its constant newness, beyond our wildest dreams and imaginings.

Like the Magi, we 'are filled with delight', gratitude and wonder. We bring along our simple gifts, not gold, frankincense or myrrh, but perhaps some bread and fish, or a couple of coins, or a jar of water, as expression of our recognition of his lordship and our surrender in worship.

The second exemplar of positive response is Joseph who, in the narrative, holds the various strands of the story together. Joseph is a dreamer, who recognises in his dreams the gentle and disturbing imperative of God's voice. The husband of Mary surrenders to each dream or angelic visitation in turn, with alacrity and completeness, following their indications to the letter without question, whatever the risk, whatever the cost. He is, of course, a Jew, the forerunner of those Jews who would follow Jesus. He, too, challenges my sensitivity, my listening, my openness to God's word, my trust in God's providential presence, saving guidance and faithful care. He invites me to allow God to direct my life rather more closely, a directing which may also have an influence on the lives and destinies of others.

2. The negative response

The negative response is powerfully delineated, and is centred in the capital, the stronghold of the Jewish leadership. The first protagonists are the powerful, the religious élite, the 'chief priests and lawyers of the Jewish people' − anticipating the passion gathering of Matthew 26:57 and 27:1. The lawyers are the experts, knowing the scriptures inside out, well able to quote chapter and verse, and to state categorically that it is in Bethlehem that the longed-for shepherd-king of the Jewish people would be born. Yet, they remain in Jerusalem, finding no incentive to journey, making no attempt to move away from where they are, refusing to search.

The people of the city share their consternation and their role of royal accomplices, evincing little interest in the new-born king, and foreshadowing their rejection of him during his passion, and their acceptance of responsibility for his death (Mt 27:25).

Then there is Herod, riddled with fear, threatened to the core of his being by these foreign visitors and their star story and talk of a rival king, clinging to power and status, clutching at security in anger, paranoia and bewilderment. Initially with cunning and blatant hypocrisy, and subsequently with passion inflamed by his being outwitted, he strikes out in a frenzy of fright and frustration to destroy the child (the same verb is used as during the passion narrative in Matthew 27:20), so as to maintain and preserve his position. Quite irrationally, and with extraordinary malice, he widens the net of slaughter to the surrounding district, and extends the age range to two years. He is a man impervious to God and God's claims.

As we reflect, we may perhaps recognise in ourselves the traits of the religious leaders in the story, that tendency towards a stolid staying: a quoting of scriptures, rules, documents or experts, whilst remaining planted in oak-firm immobility, with heart and attitudes unchanged. We may become aware of a gentle, complacent, scarce-believing, arrogant, bored or busy hesitancy or unwilling-ness to go further in search of the child, in search of light and growth and fuller life.

We may even detect something of Herod within us, a clinging to forms of power and manipulation and domi-nation, or an exaggerated sense of status. Perhaps we, too, clutch at one or other of the many sources of personal security which we have gathered around us. Maybe we are unwilling to let go of the old and welcome the new; or we are angry that things cannot be the same as they were. Perhaps we prefer to worship at our own shrine. Admittedly, we would not wish to identify with Herod in his attempt to murder the child, but we can find effective ways of silencing him. I am quite good at organising for him, from time to time, a brief or lengthy Egyptian holiday to keep him at a comfortable distance, and to avoid having to change or be more generous ... just yet!

With regard to others who walk into our worldview or stumble onto our patch, we can sometimes simulate interest whilst orchestrating tactics of evasion. We can strike out dismissively, use ridicule or sarcasm, and be destructively critical, because they have different ideas or innovative suggestions, and threaten us in one way or another. We can marginalise God's stargazing visionaries, and in so many ways hinder the advent of the kingdom. Reflecting on the image of the star should disturb all of us who exercise roles of responsibility within the Christian community.

CONCLUSION

Chapter two of Matthew's narrative is a fascinating presentation of the Good News, and reveals the author's penetrating insight into the rich mystery of God's dealings with the people, and into the person and mission of Jesus, the Christ. It is an invitation to respond in faith, to acknowledge God's ongoing presence, to accept Jesus as our saviour (Mt 1:23), and to take our place amongst the new people of God. It also constitutes an exciting challenge to us as we work out the implications of discipleship at a personal and communal level in the complexity of our lives, offering us much to ponder at each season of the year. Along with the challenge, it also brings reassurance, for 'God is with us' in all our coming and going. That presence will repeatedly cause the rising of a star, beckoning us daily.

2 | CELEBRATING AT CANA

Whenever I am involved in planning meetings or leading retreats, and quite frequently in personal prayer, I find myself drawn to retrace my steps and make the journey again to Cana-in-Galilee, for this small town which features in John's presentation of the Gospel never ceases to be for me a source of inspiration and challenge.[1]

1   This chapter is a thorough revision of an article published in *Religious Life Review*, vol 31, Jul/Aug 1992, pp. 171-175. I am grateful for permission to use this material. In the study of John, I have found the following commentaries very useful: C.K. Barrett, *The Gospel according to John* (London, SPCK 1978); R.E. Brown, *The Gospel according to John* (London, Chapmans 1972); C.H. Dodd, *The Interpretation of the Fourth Gospel* (Cambridge, CUP 1968); E. Haenchen, *John* vol 2 (Philadelphia, Fortress 1984); R.H. Lightfoot, *St John's Gospel* (Oxford, OUP 1956); B. Lindars, *The Gospel of John* (London, Oliphants 1972); J. Marsh, *St John* (London, Penguin 1968); R. Schnackenburg, *The Gospel according to St John* vol 1 (London, Burns & Oates 1968), vol 2 (1980), vol 3 (1982). I am particularly indebted to F.J. Moloney, *Belief in the Word. Reading John 1-4* (Minneapolis, Fortress Press 1993); pp. 77-92, and I. de la Potterie, *Mary in the Mystery of the Covenant* (New York, Alba House 1992), pp. 157-208. See also J.W. Pryor, *John: Evangelist of the Covenant People. The Narrative and Themes of the Fourth Gospel* (London, DLT 1992).

THE SETTING: John 2:1

The author commences the Cana story by setting the scene:

> On the third day there was a wedding at Cana in Galilee.
> The mother of Jesus was there, and Jesus and his disciples
> had also been invited (Jn 2:1-2).

He comments on the time, the occasion and the place, and introduces the main characters. The reference to Galilee links the episode with the preceding incident, the call of Philip and of Nathaniel who, we are told later, comes from Cana (Jn 21:2). Cana is a two-way town. Looking ahead, it is the location of another important narrative, the cure of the court official's son, the second of Jesus' signs, which illustrates the theme that Jesus is the source of life (Jn 4:46-54). The two Cana episodes frame a whole section of the gospel in which the evangelist treats the question of the nature of faith (Jn 2:1-4:54).[2] Looking backwards, it can be seen as the culmination of the inaugural period of Jesus' public presence. This is structured in a sequence of specifically designated 'days' during which the Baptist bears witness to him, and his first disciples are summoned.[3]

2   See F.J. Moloney, 'From Cana to Cana (John 2:1-4,54) and the Fourth
    Evangelist's Concept of Correct (and Incorrect) Faith', in *Salesianum* 40
    (1978), pp. 817-43. The two Cana narratives have a remarkably parallel
    structure: the statement of a problem (2:3; 4:46); a request (2:3; 4:47); a
    rebuke (2:4; 4:48); a reaction in which there is a reference to 'word' (2:5
    -legein; 4:50 -logos); a consequence, which is a miracle leading to the faith
    of others (2:6-11; 4:51-53).

3   The first day occupies verses 19-28; 'the next day' verses 29-34; 'the next
    day again' verses 35-42; 'the next day' verses 43-51. On this fourth day
    Jesus takes the initiative in calling Philip, and promises greater things to
    come (v 50). I. de la Potterie, *Mary*, pp. 164-170, argues strongly for the
    unity of 1:1-2:12), but maintains that there is a decisive break at 2:12. I
    prefer to follow R.E. Brown and F.J. Moloney in considering the Cana
    story as a 'bridging scene'.

The keynote of the passage is the initial phrase 'on the third day'. In Jewish tradition the third day has long been associated with the giving of the Law to Moses on Sinai (Ex 19:16), when the glory of Yahweh was manifested to the people of Israel. This gift was celebrated liturgically in the annual feast of Pentecost, which climaxed on the third day. This reference and linkage creates in the reader an expectation of something significant to follow.

From a different perspective, the third day designation is also a clue at the outset that the full meaning of the narrative can be understood only in the light of the resurrection, the Easter event.[4]

The context is a wedding celebration, an occasion of great joy and hope in the community: joy because of shared love and commitment; joy in the hope of continued life together, of fruitfulness, of a future. For the fourth evangelist, steeped in the Old Testament, such a wedding setting is pregnant with significance.

In the literature of his people the image of the wedding or espousals is a symbol of the relationship of God and the people (cf. Hos 2:19-20; Is 54:4-8; 62:4-5; Jer 2:2; Ezek 16; Song of Songs), and the wedding banquet is a favourite symbol for the eschatological banquet, the coming time of blessing and joy, the messianic days, an era which in the mind of poet and dreamer will be characterised by feasting and abundance. Frequently, the

---

4 The preparation for the feast had evolved. It now consisted in a remote three day period culminating on a fourth day, which marked the beginning of the formal mosaic triduum prior to the climax 'on the third day'. John is closely modelling his presentation along these lines. See F.J. Moloney, *Belief in the Word*, pp. 53-60. J.W. Pryor expresses reservations: *John*, pp. 16-17.

prophets take wine as the image of the joy and plenty of the 'last days', the new age, the overflowing richness of messianic deliverance and new covenant. Isaiah predicts:

> On this mountain the Lord of hosts will prepare
> a banquet of rich fare for all the peoples,
> a banquet of wines well matured,
> richest fare and well-matured wines strained clear
> (Is 25:6).

Joel imagines that when that day comes:

> the mountains will run with the new wine
> and the hills flow with milk.
> Every channel in Judah will be full of water.
> (Joel 3:18).

And according to the vision of Amos:

> A time is coming, says the Lord,
> when the ploughman will follow hard on the reaper,
> and he who treads the grapes after him who sows the seed.
> The mountains will run with fresh wine,
> and every hill will flow with it (Amos 9:13).

There is a snippet of apocalyptic literature of the time in which it is promised that each vine will have a thousand branches, each branch carry a thousand clusters, each cluster bear a thousand grapes, and each grape (coincidentally for our text) produce 120 gallons of wine.[5] Quite a festivity!

Finally, the characters are brought on stage. The first to be mentioned is the mother of Jesus, who will play a central role in the narrative. This is the first mention of her in the gospel. She will feature again at the Calvary

5   See R.E. Brown, *John*, p. 105.

scene, also in connection with the 'hour' of Jesus. About Jesus we have already learned a great deal in the previous chapter, through the witness of John the Baptist (Jn 1:19-34). He is the one who is to come (Jn 1:26), the Lamb of God (Jn 1:29), the one who is to baptise with the Holy Spirit (Jn 1:33), and the chosen one of God (Jn 1:34). We have encountered the disciples also: Andrew and his un-named companion, who are directed to Jesus by the Baptist (Jn 1:35-39); Simon Peter, whom Andrew brings along, and whom Jesus renames Cephas, meaning Rock (Jn 1:40-42); Philip from Bethsaida, whom Jesus has met and called to follow him; and Nathaniel, whom Philip has invited to 'come and see' Jesus (Jn 1:43-51). Their response to Jesus has told us even more about him: after the initial 'Rabbi' (Jn 1:38, 49), he is seen to be the messiah (Jn 1:41), the one written about by Moses in the Law and by the prophets (Jn 1:45), the Son of God and king of Israel (Jn 1:49).

These assessments and confessions remain within traditional Jewish categories. Jesus himself has promised the revelation of God in the Son of Man (Jn 1:51). Finally, we must also keep in mind what is announced in the prologue (Jn 1:1-18): that he is the enfleshment of the Word, source of light and life, the revelation of God's 'enduring love'.[6]

---

6 The word of God (*dabar*) in the Old Testament tradition can be viewed under two complementary aspects. Firstly, it has to do with understanding, enlightenment, revelation (as seen in the Law and the Prophets). Secondly, it is dynamic, creative; it directs history and is life-giving. This tradition, along with the Old Testament presentation of Wisdom, lies behind the Johannine use of the Logos. See R.E. Brown, *John*, pp. 519-524.

THE ROLE OF THE MOTHER OF JESUS:
John 2:2-6

The role of the mother of Jesus in the story is to point out a need. An embarrassing situation is developing. She notices this, is concerned, and turns to Jesus and says:

They have no wine left (Jn 2:3).

At the level of the unfolding of the story, this is simply a recognition and statement of fact, with a discreet hint that he might do something about it, but without the implication that she is expecting a miracle. At the theological level of the story, however, her comment has far-reaching implications. What she is indicating is the inadequacy of the old dispensation. The wine has run out, the supply has dried up, the whole system of Judaism is empty, barren, unproductive, atrophied. There is a profound need for something new and life-giving.

The rather abrupt response of her son has been a constant source of perplexity for reader and scholar alike:

Woman, what do you want from me? My hour has not yet come (Jn 2:5 NJB).

In itself the term 'woman' is not impolite nor an indication of disapproval or lack of affection. There are several instances of Jesus addressing women in this manner (Mt 15:28; Lk 13:12; Jn 4:21; 8:10; 20:13). It is, however, an unusual way for a son to address his mother. Jesus uses the same term on the other occasion in the fourth gospel when his mother is present, the Calvary scene (Jn 19:26). This would suggest that the title carries a deeper significance.

The phrase is literally rendered 'what is this to me and to you', and is a formula found in the Old Testament to indicate an unwillingness to become involved (cf. 2 Kings 33:13; Hos 14:9). In this context, it implies a distancing, an area of separation between Jesus and his mother. There is a lack of understanding because they are operating at different levels. The mother of Jesus is concerned with the practical problem of the current wine shortage, whereas Jesus sees the lack of wine in a different perspective, its symbolic significance in terms of his mission. There are things about Jesus and his mission of which she is unaware. She is outside the understanding of the mystery of the 'hour'. It is not for her to influence the pattern of his ministry. 'The law according to which he works is imposed on him by another.'[7] It is his Father's work that he is about. Like the other characters (and the reader), she will have to wait.

The term 'hour' recurs throughout the Johannine story as a technical term. From the enigmatic reference here in John 2:4, through the violent indications of John 7:30 and 8:20, when attempts are made to arrest him, the life of Jesus moves towards the time of the fulfilment of his mission, a time which cannot be anticipated, and which will be dictated by the Father. It is after the arrival of the Greeks at the festival that Jesus proclaims:

> The hour has come for the Son of Man to be glorified (Jn 12:33).

And in what is the Johannine equivalent of the synoptic agony scene, he continues:

---

7   R. Schnackenburg, *St John*, p. 329. Misunderstanding is a technique which the evangelist uses on other occasions to move from one level of meaning to another, and to pave the way for further revelation (see the Nicodemus story [3:1-6], and the incident with the woman at the well [4:7-15]). In the Synoptics too, Jesus places himself beyond family relationships when it is a question of his mission (see Lk 2:49; 11:27-28; Mk 3:33-35).

Now my soul is in turmoil, and what am I to say? 'Father, save me from this hour'? No, it was for this that I came to this hour. Father, glorify your name (Jn 12:27).

At the Supper it becomes clear that the hour consists in Jesus' passing from this world to the Father (Jn 13:1). Through his returning to the Father by means of his being uplifted on the cross and through his resurrection/ ascension, his glory (that is, his identity as Son, unique revealer and source of life), is manifested. In the hour are revealed the love of God for the world in the giving of the Son (Jn 3:15-16), the love of Jesus for his Father in his obedient surrender, and the love for his own (Jn 13:1). It is in this supreme moment of the hour, when Jesus has completed his task and returned to the Father, that the new wine can flow in messianic abundance and fullness through the giving of the Spirit.[8]

The reaction of the Mother of Jesus to his unexpected reply is to address the servants:

'Do whatever he tells you' (Jn 2:5).

She directs them to her son. Her injunction evinces a profound and unconditional trust in his word, in spite of his seeming refusal. As far as the story goes, she has no evidence on which to base her belief in the efficacy of his word. She simply believes in him. She is the first person in the narrative to commit herself completely to his word, and she thus exemplifies the true meaning of

---

8   See F.J. Moloney, *The Word Became Flesh* (Dublin, Mercier 1977), pp. 101-111; R.E. Brown, *John*, pp. 517-518. I. de la Potterie, on the other hand, prefers to interpret the comment about the 'hour' as a question: 'Has not my hour already come?' This implies that the 'hour' of Jesus actually begins here, the 'hour' of his messianic revelation, which then continues throughout the public ministry and will 'attain its total accomplishment in the mystery of the Cross and of the Resurrection' (*Mary*, p. 188).

faith for the fourth evangelist. There is also a link between her words here and the words of the people assembled at Sinai who, on receiving the law from Moses, solemnly commit themselves to Yahweh in the words:

'Whatever Yahweh has said, we will do' (Ex 19:8).

This is a covenant formula, an expression of the people's faith commitment and obedience pledge to Yahweh. The final words of the mother of Jesus in this episode, and also in the whole gospel, take this up and re-express it in terms of trusting surrender to the word of Jesus.

A reflection on the story so far

The first aspect of the role of the mother of Jesus is to point out a need. Her action makes me wonder which area of poverty and need she would indicate in my own life and in the life of the community to which I belong. The Cana couple had no alternative than to recognise and acknowledge the predicament in which they found themselves. The cups were empty, there was no gainsaying that. The situation could not be hidden or glossed over or explained away. But *we* can be blind. Fear, complacency, tunnel-vision, the ostrich syndrome, busy-ness can prevent us from noticing, from being open to reality. We need to become poor enough and free enough to recognise and to own our need. The twinning of truth and trust has enormous potential for change and growth. I believe that the mother of Jesus is still there, is with us in our prayer, and that she will help us see our need. It may be as obvious as an empty wine glass − or it may not.

The statement: 'there is no wine left', strikes a chord in me. There are times in my own faith journey and ministry when this description fits me to a T. The sparkle has gone, the zest and lightness of step have disappeared. There seems little to show and nothing more to offer. Drive, energetic outreach, innovative thinking have locked solid.

As religious, and as Church, we are all aware of falling numbers and rising median age. We are conscious of weariness and struggle, and of the many problems facing us in our evangelising mission. The thought may occur that the wine, though it may not yet have entirely run out, is certainly in shorter supply, and may have lost something of its bouquet and taste; that aspects of the old dispensation, old ways of thinking and praying and worshipping, old ways of fulfilling our mission are now unattractive, dissatisfying, unfruitful, no longer life-giving. Festivity can seem hollow. Perhaps we are into funerals rather than weddings!

I believe that it can be good for me, good for us, to spend time holding and gazing into an empty glass, in the acknowledgement and owning of reality, grieving if necessary – rather like the Emmaus disciples ('we had hoped…') – in disappointment and some confusion, in disillusionment, perhaps, and fear for the future; above all in humble truth.

This is not an invitation to melancholy and despair in personal or communal mid-life! It is an invitation, rather, to enter the experience of Passover, the experience of the hour. For the role of the mother of Jesus in the narrative, as we have seen, has two aspects: having pointed out the need, she goes on to indicate the remedy. She sends the servants to her son. He is the only one who can do anything to salvage the situation. She invites us to make space and call him in.

The first beatitude is understood by Barclay in terms of the recognition of our great helplessness and the placing of our utter trust in God.[9] The mother of Jesus shows the way to such radical trust in the efficacy of the presence and word of her son: 'Do whatever he tells you'. An empty wine glass can remain empty on a table, a cupboard shelf or a bar. It can be discarded, shattered to tiny fragments on a stone floor. Or, because it stands empty, and precisely because it stands empty, it can be filled.

THE RESPONSE OF JESUS: John 2:7-10

As we return to the narrative and to the main action of the story, we find that the imagery shifts slightly. Jesus orders the servants to fill the six large stone jars with water.

The jars are meant for ablutions; stone was thought not to contract ritual contamination. The fact that there are six is probalby intended to signify that the world of Jewish ritual is lacking in perfection since, in that culture, seven was thought to be the perfect number.

Although filling jars with water would appear to be an odd solution to a wine shortage, the servants do not demur. The woman has told them to comply with his instructions, with his word, and so they do, and they fill them to the brim. Jesus then speaks a second word; he tells them to draw some off and take a sample to the chief steward. Again they obey. The water is found to be wine, and there is far, far more than they know what to do with,

9   W. Barclay, *The Gospel of Matthew* vol 1 (Edinburgh, St Andrew's Press 1956), p. 87.

120 gallons in fact. The experienced steward quickly notes, not without surprise and a little indignation, that the wine is of a vastly superior vintage. Naturally, he is keen to identify its source.

In John's theology, all this illustrates the conviction that the wedding dreams of Israel are now fulfilled, the banquet is inaugurated, the messianic age has dawned, has had its beginning. It indicates that the new life of the new era ushered in by Jesus is far richer, more abundant, and of immeasurably finer quality than the old. It is a matter of wine instead of water. 'If only you knew the gift of God...' (Jn 4:10). The gift which Jesus offers surpasses by far the gift of the Jewish Law and ritual and traditions. As we read in the Prologue:

> Indeed, from his fullness we have, all of us,
> received – one gift replacing another,
> for the Law was given through Moses,
> grace and truth have gone through Jesus Christ.
> No one has ever seen God;
> it is the only Son, who is close to the Father's heart,
> who has made him known (Jn 1:16-18).

The replacement of the water in the ritual purification jars by the finest of wines introduces a theme which will be pursued throughout the gospel, as Jesus systematically gives new meaning to the feasts and institutions of Israel. Wine, which was one of the favourite sapiential symbols for the Law, now becomes the symbol of the revelation and truth which Jesus brings.

It is important not to overlook the fact that this transformation has been brought about as a result of the trust of the mother and the obedient compliance of the servants. The action revolves around the world.

CONCLUSION OF THE NARRATIVE:
John 2:11-12

The evangelist draws the narrative to a conclusion by remarking that this was the first of Jesus' signs.[10] John prefers to designate the miracles or mighty works of Jesus in this way. They are symbols which point to his identity; they indicate what he is about; they are revelation. However, the term has a wider significance than 'miracle'. Ordinary things like water can be 'signs'; they have great symbolic potential and value. Events or actions can also be signs. Signs give access to something greater than themselves; they open windows onto mystery. This Cana sign, then, revealed his glory, and led his disciples to believe in him. Again there is a link with the Sinai event in which the glory of Yahweh was manifested (Ex 19:1), a revelation superseded by the epiphany of God's glory in the presence and activity of Jesus, the glory of the Father's only Son (Jn 1:14) — one gift instead of another (Jn 1:16). The replacement of water by wine, and the abundance of choice wine to fill a deficiency, a void, is a sign which reveals to the disciples his identity and role as messiah: the manifestation of the saving presence of Yahweh.

A further dimension of this theme is suggested by the wedding setting, which is the fundamental symbol. In the course of the narrative we never encounter the bridegroom; we merely hear him reprimanded as the one responsible for keeping the good wine till now. The bride does not even get a mention. It seems to some scholars

---

10 For an excellent treatment of 'Signs', see R.E. Brown, *John*, pp. 525-532. I. de la Potterie, *Mary*, pp. 177-181 makes some very perceptive comments on the subject.

that Jesus takes the place of the bridegroom, and at the
theological level of the story becomes the true bridegroom
of the narrative. The term reappears in John 3:29-30,
where John the Baptist applies it to Jesus:

> It is the bridegroom who marries the bride. The bride-
> groom's friend, who stands by and listens to him, is over-
> joyed at hearing the bridegroom's voice. This is my joy,
> and now it is complete. He must grow greater; I must
> become less.

Jesus reveals himself at Cana as the messianic bridegroom,
entering into a new and definite covenant relationship
with the new people of God.[11]

The disciples' itinerary of growth in understanding and
faith has now reached a certain level of maturation, as
they respond to the revelation of Jesus in the sign which
is Cana. We remain, nevertheless, under the shadow of
the 'not yet' of John 2:4. Cana is a foreshadowing, a
proleptic manifestation, a pointer; it is the beginning of
the signs. It is only when the hour of Jesus finally comes
that his glory will be fully revealed and the new life of
the Spirit will freely flow. Through the supreme sign of
the resurrection (on the third day) the disciples will receive
the gift of complete faith in him.

Finally, Jesus and his mother, the disciples (and his
'brothers', who will reappear in John 7:1-10), leave Cana
and move to Capernaum, as the ministry of Jesus
continues.

Reference was made earlier to the symbolism attached
to the Mother of Jesus being addressed as woman, a term
adopted also in the Calvary scene. Jesus is now assuming

---

11 See I. de la Potterie, *Mary*, pp. 196-201; F.J. Moloney, *Belief in the Word*,
    pp. 86-87

his messianic role, and the relationship between them is no longer simply that of mother and son. A new perspective is being opened up, and she is drawn into his saving mission. In the prophets there is a symbolic woman, referred to as the Daughter of Zion, Mother-Zion, Virgin Israel. Israel's hope for salvation was projected upon this symbolic figure. In Mary this hope is realised in history. She is both the mother of Jesus and the Daughter of Zon, the representative of the people from whom Jesus comes, the personification of this symbol. She is at the heart of a major feminine messianic thread.[12] Links are also being made with the woman who, in the Book of Revelation, brings forth the messiah and who, along with her other offspring, is attacked by the dragon (Rev 12:1-6). This reference is to be seen against the background of Genesis 3:15, the woman, Eve, whose offspring will be at enmity with the serpent. It is in connection with the presence of the mother of Jesus at the cross, when his hour finally comes (Jn 19:25-27), that this symbolism is clarified. There she is the new Eve, the symbol of the Church, and is 'entrusted with offspring whom she must protect in the continuing struggle between Satan and the followers of the messiah'.[13] At Cana there is the first indication of her association in this hour.

Some reflections on the rest of the narrative

Often, at the end of the day, I go to Jesus with the stone water jar which is me. Sometimes the water seems clear

---

12 See I. de la Potterie, *Mary*, pp. 202-205, and also xxiii-xl.
13 R.E. Brown, *John*, p. 109; he discusses this issue on pp. 107-109.

and fresh, like the spilling falls and fast-flowing streams of the Lake District, where I like to walk. At other times it is stale and stagnant and muddied. It is the water of my story: what I have become; what I have done; the gifts I have; the love I have given and received; the inadequacies and weaknesses, mistakes and mess, too.

As families, church and religious communities, we can approach him together, bringing our water jars, our communal story. Inspired and encouraged by the Mother of Jesus, we come in simplicity, trusting in the efficacy of the word of her son. We believe that in his enduring love he can transform the water of our lives into wine, beyond our wildest dreams and imaginings. We know that he can give new and abundant life, and a future which is rich and fruitful. We may even dare to hope that he has kept the best wine until now.

The now of the fulfilment of Israel's dreams has arrived in Jesus. He is the messianic bridegroom, who inaugurates the new covenant and brings into existence the new people of God. Through our baptism, our receiving the gift of the Spirit (Jn 19:30; 20:22-23), we are caught up in this new era, drawn into the new covenant relationship with God in Christ. We are a banqueting people. The lavish love of God inundates us with gifts. The focal point of this new era and the turning point of history is the hour of Jesus. Easter is the supreme expression of the Father's faithful love for Jesus, the obedient one. And in the risen one, through the outpouring of the Spirit, Easter is the expression and pledge of the Father's enduring love for us. Easter is celebration time, new life time, when water becomes wine and empty glasses overflow. As individuals and as Church, perhaps we need to rediscover the wonder and joy of Cana, the gift which is Cana. Our God can still make all things new, and do a new thing never thought of before (Is 43:19). God's so doing may well require new wineskins, and demand new arrangements, and management and marketing skills too!

The invitation to the Cana celebration draws us into the total experience of the hour, and that hour must be willingly embraced. For us, like the Mother of Jesus, it will entail a dying. For:

> In very truth I tell you, unless a grain of wheat falls into the ground and dies, it remains that and nothing more; but if it dies, it bears a rich harvest (Jn 12:24).

Her dying, her not totally understanding, her surrender in trust to the word of Jesus, enabled the new wine to flow. Her commitment to the word of her son (her authentic faith in the Johannine sense), led to a situation in which the disciples were brought to believe. This Cana invitation challenges us to do whatever he tells you, a pattern which will lead us to fuller life (Jn 10:10), and will draw others into that experience.

3 | THE LITTLE PEOPLE

As we wander through the pages of Mark's Gospel, following the hectic journeying of Jesus, we encounter a wide variety of people. Many scripture commentators highlight the way in which this evangelist treats the close disciples of Jesus; and this is a favourite theme of mine too.[1] The religious authorities feature prominently in the dénouement of the narrative, and it is fascinating to follow their intensifying conflict with Jesus.[2]

However, I would like to reflect with you on those whom two American writers, Rhoads and Michie, call the little people in Mark. These individuals (technically they do not form a group) appear briefly on the stage and then quickly exit, but they play a significant role in the story, and they exemplify the genuine values of the kingdom,

1 See M.T. Winstanley, *Come and See* (London, DLT 1985) pp. 100-110.
2 See J.D. Kingsbury, *Conflict in Mark, – Jesus, Authorities, Disciples* (Minneapolis, Fortress Press 1989).

values which are alien to the authorities, and which the disciples themselves struggle to embrace.[3]

These little people include Simon's mother-in-law (Mk 1:29-31), the leper (Mk 1:40-45), the men who bring the paralytic to Jesus (Mk 2:1-12), Jairus and his daughter and the woman with a haemorrhage (Mk 5:21-43), the Syrophoenician woman (Mk 7:24-30), Bartimaeus (Mk 10:46-52) and, in the later part of the Gospel, the widow in the Temple (Mk 12:41-44); the woman who anoints Jesus (Mk 14:3-9), Simon of Cyrene (Mk 15:21), the women at Calvary (Mk 15:40-41) and at the tomb (Mk 16:1-2), and Joseph of Arimathaea (Mk 15:42-47) – such a rich mélange of personalities. Some of these people come to Jesus seeking healing for others in need, or for themselves. Others feature in a context of service.[4]

3   D. Rhoads and D. Michie, *Mark as Story* (Philadelphia, Fortress Press 1982), pp. 192ff. J.D. Kingsbury, *Conflict in Mark*, pp. 24-27, refers to the wide variety of the minor characters in the narrative. Some are so unobtrusive that they meld into the setting (like Simon in 14:3). Others simply facilitate the action of an episode, like Herodias in 6:14-19. Others serve merely as catalysts, like the man with the withered hand in 3:1-6. There are, however, some characters who play a greater role. For some, like Barabbas or the soldiers in the Passion narrative, this is of a rather negative kind. For others the role is positive: they stand out for the quality of their faith and trust, or because they convey the meaning of service. These would correspond to the Little People of Rhoads and Michie.

4   I have found helpful the commentaries on Mark's Gospel by H. Anderson, *The Gospel of Mark* (London, Oliphants 1976); C.E.B. Cranfield, *The Gospel according to St Mark* (Cambridge, CUP 1977);. W. Harrington, *Mark* (Dublin, Veritas 1979); M.D. Hooker, *The Gospel according to St Mark* (London, A & C Black 1991); W.L. Lane, *The Gospel of Mark* (Grand Rapids, Eerdmans 1974); D.E. Nineham, *St Mark* (London, Penguin Books 1963); E. Schweizer, *The Good News according to Mark* (London, SPCK 1971); V. Taylor, *The Gospel according to St Mark* (London, Macmillan 1957). Also: F. Mussner, *The Miracles of Jesus* (Shannon, Ecclesia Press 1970); F.J. Moloney, 'Jesus and Woman' in F. Bergamelli and M. Cimosa (eds) *Virgo Fidelis, Studi Mariani* (Rome, Edizioni Liturgiche 1988); pp. 53-80; E.S. Fiorenza, *In Memory of Her* (London, SCM 1983); J. Reilly, *Praying Mark* (Sydney, ST PAULS 1992).

FAITH AT THE SERVICE OF OTHERS

1. The friends of the paralytic: Mark 2:1-12

Amongst those who come to Jesus seeking healing for another, the friends of the paralytic are apt to be the most easily overlooked, since the focus of the story is the interaction between Jesus and the sufferer, the Lord's healing and forgiving words, and the conflict which flares up between Jesus and the religious leaders. Clearly, the four are deeply committed to their friend and are determined to get him to Jesus. Finding their way into the house blocked by the thronging crowds,

> they made an opening in the roof over the place where Jesus was, and when they had broken through they lowered the bed on which the paralysed man was lying (Mk 2:4).

The roof would probably have consisted of crossbeams overlaid with a matting of branches and hardened mud. Access would have been by means of an outside stairway. They show initiative and ingenuity, and great faith in the power and the compassion of Jesus.

He, for his part, is not slow to recognise this trust and, I suspect, their affection and concern for their unfortunate friend, their willingness to put themselves out on his behalf. When he saw *their* faith, he proclaimed the man's sins forgiven, and later cured him of his affliction. They must have shared the wonder and joy of the onlookers when he got up from his stretcher, picked it up, and walked out of the house.[5]

5 For further reflections on the paralytic, see M.T. Winstanley, *Come and See*, pp. 74-82.

2. Jairus and his daughter: Mark 5:22-24 and 35-43

One of the most emotional scenes in Mark's Gospel is, I believe, that in which Jesus is approached at the lakeside by Jairus, the president of the local synagogue, a member of the Jewish establishment.[6] In a manner hardly appropriate for one of his standing, but which betrays the depth of his distress, he throws himself at Jesus' feet, and pleads:

> 'My little daughter is at death's door. I beg you to come and lay your hands on her so that her life may be saved' (Mk 5:23).

Having successfully pleaded with Jesus that he accompany him to his home, he is confronted en route with a message that his daughter has in fact died, implying that there is no point in troubling the Master further; all hope has been lost. Somehow, Jairus finds it within himself, despite the odds and the pressure, to respond to Jesus' invitation: 'Do not be afraid; *keep on* believing'. On their reaching the house, Jesus is unperturbed by all the commotion or by the incredulous laughter of the onlookers. Having excluded the crowd, he takes Jairus and his wife and his three disciples into the room in which the girl is lying. With great tenderness, Jesus takes her by the hand, calls her back to life and restores her to her

---

6   The stories of the raising to life of Jairus' daughter and the cure of the woman with the haemorrhage really belong together. They are linked structurally by the Markan literary device of framing or sandwiching, one being used as an interlude within the other. They are also connected thematically through their concern with the topics of faith and life. Each is to be understood in the light of the other. (See F.J. Moloney, *art. cit.*, pp. 58-59). They form the climax of the series of miracles or 'mighty works', which in crescendo runs from 4:35-5:43, and which illustrates the authority of Jesus.

mother and father, suggesting that she be given something to eat. The reader is meant to appreciate, also, the deeper import of the words, save and live, which Jairus used in his initial request.

3. The Syro-Phoenician woman: Mark 7:24-30

The next episode for our reflection is for me one of the most powerful and moving expressions of poverty of spirit to be found in the New Testament. It is the story of the Syro-Phoenician woman, who approaches Jesus seeking a cure for her daughter. As his geographical indications suggest (Mk 7:24 and 31), it is particularly significant for the evangelist that the incident occurs in Gentile territory, even though in Jesus' time the area of upper Galilee was Gentile only in a limited sense.

Mark prefaces the story with the comment that Jesus has found a house in which to stay so as to remain unrecognised! Perhaps he felt the need for some privacy.

As usual, his presence does not go unnoticed, and this Gentile woman gets to hear that he is in the vicinity and searches him out. She enters the house and falls at his feet as a suppliant, begging him to drive the unclean spirit out of her daughter. Her pleading is a recognition of her plight, and an expression of her trust in his power and willingness to help her. As the first Gentile to make such a request, she introduces an air of suspense into the narrative's unfolding.

Jesus makes that puzzling reply:

> 'Let the children be satisfied first; it is not right to take the children's bread and throw it to the dogs' (Mk 7:27).

It seems a rather harsh answer, suggesting that Jesus saw
his mission as confined to the Gentiles. His miracles are
closely linked with his preaching, since they are a sign
and an expression of the kingdom's inbreaking, and can
occur only where there is faith. The woman's request
seems to fall outside this context.[7] Yet she is undeterred
and replies:

> 'Sir, even the dogs under the table eat the children's
> scraps' (Mk 7:28).

The woman accepts what Jesus says; she accepts the
analogy and its implications, acknowledging that Israel
has priority in God's saving plan. She recognises that she
has no rights, no claims to assistance; that she cannot
merit a cure, is utterly empty-handed, totally dependent;
but she still trusts that he will do what she asks.

It is not just a question of persistence fuelled by her
need and deep concern for her daughter. Nor is it simply
that her womanly intuition senses from the look in his
eyes, or the tone of his voice, that he is a man of immense
compassion. Her reply also indicates some glimmering
of understanding concerning the kingdom, the recognition
'that the children are already being fed, and that, in spite
of their recognised priority, there is hope for her now'.[8]
She moves in a context of faith, perceiving the presence
of God's power in Jesus. This he recognises, and grants
her request, assuring her that when she reaches home
again, she will find her daughter restored. She takes him
at his word, and returns to her home, where she finds
her daughter liberated from her affliction. She is a woman
of remarkable faith.

---

7   See M.D. Hooker, *St Mark*, pp. 182-3.
8   M.D. Hooker *St Mark*, p. 182.

Perhaps this little person plays an important role in Jesus' growing awareness of his mission, broadening out to that wider perspective envisaged for the servant of Yahweh by the prophet Isaiah (49:6). She certainly plays a key role in the narrative. Her faith stands in stark contrast to the legalism and self-righteousness of Judaism, which is illustrated in the section of the gospel leading up to the story (Mk 7:1-23), a section in which Jesus has challenged and upturned some fundamental Jewish tenets. Mark's readers would see this episode as the tip of the iceberg, the initial penetration of Jewish exclusivism, the breaching of the barrier referred to in Ephesians 2:14. 'If Jesus yielded to the cry of faith while the Jew/Gentile division still stood, how much more should the Christian Church go out to the Gentiles.'[9]

CONCLUSION

Each of these three narratives illustrates not only extraordinary trust in Jesus, a trust capable of overcoming daunting obstacles, but also a profound degree of self-forgetfulness, a love which loses self in the care and service of others.

FAITH WHICH WINS HEALING

1. The leper: Mark 1:40-45

In the course of Mark's narrative there are several instances of people approaching Jesus personally for a cure. One

9   W. Harrington, *Mark*, p. 105.

of my favourites is the story of the leper. His infirmity, whether it was leprosy in the technical medical sense, or a similar unpleasant skin disease, was thought to be incurable, and entailed segregation from the social and religious life of the community. Leprosy was considered evidence of, and punishment for sin, and so a leper was deemed unclean in a religious sense also. This outcast approaches Jesus, disregarding the regulations, and apparently failing to give the customary warning. He falls to his knees at Jesus' feet and, in his isolation and hopelessness, implies his help:

'If only you want to, you can make me clean' (Mk 1:40).

Jesus is moved to compassion.[10] He bridges the dreadful chasm of separation by reaching out and touching him. Ignoring the risk of contagion and incurring the stigma of ritual defilement according to the law, Jesus responds to his trust. He makes him whole, restores him to the life of his community, and draws him into personal companionship.

'Of course I want to! Be cured' (Mk 1:41).

2. The woman suffering from a flow of blood: Mark 5:25-34

Another exquisite narrative is the story of the woman who has been suffering from haemorrhages for twelve years.

10 The majority of manuscripts attest Jesus' compassion. Other manuscripts have: 'moved with anger', 'with warm indignation', and because this is the more difficult reading, it is generally considered to be the more original. The anger of Jesus is directed against the power of evil which holds people bound.

ERRATA

Acknowledgements. p.9, line 6. *W.T.* should read *M.T.*

Contents.   chap. 7 should read *Jerusalem Gardens*.

Introduction.   p.15, line 12: *the* should read *these*.

Chapter 2:   p.35 footnote 4 should be a paragraph higher.

        p.43 line 16, *probalby* to read *probably*.

        p.44 last line: *world* to read *'word'*. ***

        p.46 line 11: *definite* to read *definitive*.

        p.46 line 8: *Zon* to read *Zion*.

Chapter 3:   p.56 line 2: *Gentiles* to read *Israel*. ***

        p.60/61 two lines are repeated.

Chapter 4:   p.69 line 12: *now* to read *not*. ***

        p.88 line 2: *evalute* to read *evaluate*.

Chapter 6:   p.128 line 17: omit brackets and insert *in* before the reference.

        p.133 line 10, in the reference, for 9 read 19.

        p.135: the second and third quotations should be in smaller print.

Chapter 7:   p.139, 141 etc: the heading should read *Jerusalem*, as on p.137.

        p.148, lines 1 and 2, omit commas.

        p.153, line 6: *referrd* to read *referred*.

     'usion: p.176, line 4, in the reference *Jn* to read *Lk*.

She seems to have done the rounds of the medical profession to no avail, and this has drained her financial resources. It is clear that her situation is quite hopeless and is even deteriorating; there is nowhere else to turn. Her distress is compounded by the fact that her ailment was considered to render her ritually unclean, and thus an outcast.

Having become aware of Jesus' reputation, she comes up from behind and touches his cloak, convinced that this would suffice for a cure. In doing so, given her condition and the blood taboo, she runs the risk of considerable disapproval. She obviously has faith in Jesus, faith of a kind, tinged perhaps with a little superstition, believing that because he is a holy man, his healing power can freely flow at a mere touch. And she is proved right; she is cured on the spot.

She is not, however, allowed to melt back into the crowd. One of the aspects of this incident which appeals to me very strongly is the way in which Jesus moved from anonymity to personal encounter through his awareness of having been touched.

His question, 'Who touched me?', which is greeted rather insensitively by the disciples, draws the woman to come forward and acknowledge what has happened to her. She fell at his feet and told him the whole truth. Jesus can now relate to her personally, and speak to her with great warmth, and respect, and affection:

> 'My daughter, your faith has restored you to health; go in peace and be free of your complaint' (Mk 5:34).

The Greek word is 'save', implying that along with the physical (and social) cure comes the offer, the gift of salvation. Peace is more than freedom from embarrass-

ment and anxiety. It connotes the wholeness and completeness of life, which derives from being drawn into
relationship with the Lord.[11]

3. Bartimaeus: Mark 10:46-52

Then there is Bartimaeus, the blind beggar, seated at the
roadside outside Jericho, as Jesus and his disciples and
a large crowd leave town. On hearing that it is Jesus who
is passing by, he determines to seize his opportunity and
cries out: 'Son of David, Jesus, have pity on me!' The
crowds who are milling round tell him to hold his tongue.
Far from being dissuaded, he cries out for mercy all the
more loudly and insistently. Jesus stops and has
Bartimaeus called to him. The man's trust and hope are
palpable as he throws off his cloak (or, if it is lying on
the ground to receive donations, he pushes it aside as
irrelevant), and springs up and comes to Jesus. Jesus puts
that gently provocative question:

'What do you want me to do for you?'

(And the reply comes unhesitatingly and predictably):

---

11 I mentioned earlier that the stories of the raising of Jairus' daughter and
the cure of the woman with the haemorrhage are linked or paired. One
element which is common is the detail that the child is twelve years old,
and the woman's affliction has been troubling her for twelve years, debarring
her medically and socially from childbearing. (See M.D. Hooker, *St Mark*,
pp. 147-150.17-150). 'The girl of twelve years of age − now marriageable
− gets up and walks. She rises to womanhood. The young woman, who
now begins to pour forth her life in menstruation, and the older woman
who experiences menstruation as a pathological condition, are both restored.
They are "given" new life' (F.J. Moloney, *art. cit.*, p.61). E.S. Fiorenza,
In Memory of Her, pp. 122-124, suggests that the lifegiving powers of women
are restored in Jesus, so that women can 'go and live in Shalom, in the
well-being and happiness of God's reigning presence, which has touched
their lives in Jesus of Nazareth'.

'What do you want me to do for you?'

(And the reply comes unhesitatingly and predictably):

'I want my sight back' (Mk 10:51).

Bartimaeus is cured because of his trust, and he follows Jesus on the road to Jerusalem – a symbol of discipleship. His faith, even if the title son of David is not entirely adequate, sets him apart from the crowd, who are not able to see the truth about Jesus. It also stands in contrast to the failure of the disciples in the previous incident, who show such little insight into the true identity and role of Jesus.[12]

CONCLUSION

These three narratives illustrate very powerfully the kingdom value of trust. They also show the gentleness and compassion of Jesus as he reaches out to the little people, who realise their need, turn to him, and so are open to receive his gift.

One element of Jesus' compassion is his reaching out to touch, an element which would have shocked the religious élite. He touches the physically and religiously unclean leper. He takes the hand of Jairus' daughter and raises her from her bed; she is dead (and so unclean), and is also of marriageable age. He is touched by the woman with vaginal bleeding; in fact, the word touch occurs three times in Mark 5:28-31, and is clearly a key

---

12 Bartimaeus is the last person in the gospel to be cured. His story is told in parallel with the (two-stage) healing of the other blind man whom people brought to Jesus in the village of Bethsaida (8:22-26).

concept. As we shall see in the next section of this chapter, he takes the hand of Simon's mother-in-law, and he allowed himself to be anointed by another woman. It was unheard of for a respected rabbi to take a woman's hand, or touch her, or be touched by her, especially in public, and the gesture was open to misinterpretation. Jesus shows remarkable freedom, as he breaks through cultural, social and religious barriers, and ritual taboos, to be close to those in need and bring them wholeness and life.

SERVICE

1. Simon's mother-in-law: Mark 1:29-31

One facet of Mark's teaching on discipleship which is brought out by the little people is that of losing self and serving. We have seen this already in some of the narratives which we have considered.

The theme is introduced right at the outset of the gospel when, within the framework of the opening day of ministry, and after the scene-setting visit to the synagogue, Jesus and his early followers go to the house of Simon and Andrew and find Simon's mother-in-law sick with fever. Jesus took hold of her hand, and raised her to her feet. Her response to her cure was to wait on them at table, even though it was the sabbath.

In that culture, it was unacceptable that a man, especially a rabbi, should be served at table by a woman. Perhaps she realised that if Jesus was free to take her hand and heal her on the sabbath, she was free to serve and care for others, a very perceptive insight into the priorities of the kingdom.

2. The widow in the temple: Mark 12:38-44

This story concludes a series of conflicts between Jesus and the religious leaders, after his entry into Jerusalem. The chief priests and the scribes and the elders question his authority (Mk 11:27). Jesus pronounces the indictment parable about the wicked tenants of the vineyard, clearly directed at them (Mk 12:1-12). The Pharisees and Herodians raise the question of the tax paid to Caesar (Mk 12:14-17), and the Sadducees the issue of the resurrection (Mk 12:18-27). Jesus then attacks the scribes, who seek to be held in respect, and wish to have the places of honour, but who 'eat up the property of widows, while for appearance' sake they say long prayers' (Mk 12:40). The hypocrisy and muddled values of the religious élite are exposed and contrasted by any action of the poor widow.

Many people were coming along to make their contribution to the Temple, throwing considerable sums into the trumpet-shaped chests which served as alms boxes. The poor widow, without power and status in society, came along and put in a couple of small coins, a very tiny amount. Yet, this was all that she had to live on, and she could have legitimately halved the amount. Jesus calls his disciples over and points this out to them very clearly. She illustrates the true meaning of worship and discipleship: losing self, giving all.

3. The woman who annoints Jesus: Mark 14:3-9

As the gospel narrative draws towards its climax, the theme of service is focused more on the person of Jesus. Its clearest and most dramatic exponent is the woman who

enters the house of Simon the leper in Bethany, when
he is entertaining Jesus to dinner. Again, Jesus is associating with an outsider. This unnamed woman brings with
her a small bottle of costly perfume, pure oil of nard.
This she breaks open and pours the oil over his head.
She shows courage in bursting into men's company and
disregarding convention. She shows generosity in breaking
the flask open so that it cannot be used again, and
lavishing its expensive contents on Jesus. Her gift, like
that of the widow, is total. Perhaps she shows a level of
insightful faith in his messiahship by anointing his head.
Above all, she shows great love and self-forgetfulness and
disinterested service. Her action is misunderstood. Those
present react angrily, complaining about the waste which
could have been used for the poor (its value would amount
to a year's wages), and they turned upon her with fury.

Jesus recognises her devotion, the spontaneity of her
kindness, her trust, and total commitment, and he springs
to her defence:

> 'Leave her alone. Why make trouble for her? It is a fine
> thing she has done for me' (Mk 14:6).

In other situations her behaviour may have been rightly
construed as wild extravagance, but Jesus is a very special
person beyond normal categories, as the woman realises,
and this is a very special moment as the hour approaches,
though of this she is not aware. He then graciously gives
her gesture a new symbolism and significance: it is the
equivalent of anointing his body for burial. In fact, after
his death, Jesus was buried hurriedly according to Mark's
version, without the customary anointing. The attempt
to do so after the sabbath was over, was foiled by God's
raising him from death. She will always be remembered
for her prophetic act, always linked with the heart of the

Good News for, through her story, is proclaimed the death and resurrection of Jesus.

Morna Hooker points out another significance of the story for Mark. Jesus has recently entered the city of Jerusalem as king. Shortly, he will be challenged by the High Priest about his messiahship (Mk 14:61), tried by Pilate as king of the Jews (Mk 15:13) and mocked as such by the soldiers (Mk 15:18). His cross will carry this inscription (Mk 15:26), and as he hangs there, his adversaries will taunt him as 'Christ, the king of Israel' (Mk 15:32). The centurion will recognise him in death as the 'Son of God' (Mk 15:39).

For Mark, the themes of death and kingship are closely connected: it is through death that Jesus is revealed as the messiah, the anointed one. 'It seems likely that he interpreted this anointing for burial as the symbol of Jesus' messianic anointing also.

The fact that the ritual was performed by a woman rather than a priest is just one more anomaly in a story that is already anomalous from beginning to end.[13]

The depth of the woman's devotion is highlighted by means of a typically Markan literary device. The evangelist precedes the incident by a note that the religious leaders sought to devise a cunning plan to seize Jesus and put him to death (Mk 14:1). He follows it immediately by reference to Judas' agreement with them to betray him (Mk 14:10). The twofold contrast is quite breathtaking.

---

13 M.D. Hooker, *St Mark*, p. 328.

3. Friends during the passion: Mark 15:21-47

As we move into the passion narrative, we encounter
Simon of Cyrene, a pilgrim or repatriated diaspora Jew,
who is pressed into service to carry Jesus' crossbeam (Mk
15:21). On Calvary we find a number of women present,
'watching from a distance' (Mk 15:40). Among them were
Mary of Magdala, Mary the mother of James the younger,
and Salome,

> who had all followed him and looked after him when
> he was in Galilee, and there were many others who had
> come up to Jerusalem with him (Mk 15:41).

The phrasing, which links following, being with, and
serving, is significant, particularly in this passion context.

After Jesus' death, Joseph of Arimathaea was given leave
to see to his burial.

> He bought a linen sheet, took him down from the cross,
> and wrapped him in the sheet. Then he laid him in a
> tomb cut out of rock, and rolled a stone against the
> entrance (Mk 15:46).

Given his position as a respected member of the Council,
this man showed great courage in seeking permission to
bury Jesus and then in actually doing so. The one act
of service which the onset of the sabbath had prevented
him from performing, the women sought to supply early
on the Sunday morning, bringing aromatic oils to anoint
the body of Jesus. Once again, they show their characteristic devotion and self-forgetfulness.

It is interesting to note that Mark emphasises this theme
of service in the second half of his Gospel. Jesus goes
to great lengths to inculcate this value. It epitomises his
style of messiahship and must therefore be the characteristic of genuine discipleship.

> Among you, whoever wants to be great must be your
> servant, and whoever wants to be first must be the slave
> of all. For the Son of Man did not come to be served
> but to serve, and to give his life as a ransom for many
> (Mk 10:44-45; cf. 8:34-38; 9:33-37).

The twelve consistently fail to understand and to accept
this.[14] By contrast, the little people seem to understand
almost instinctively, and exemplify in their living, what
Jesus is really about. It is no less interesting to observe
that in the end the little people perform for Jesus the
services which his disciples ought to have rendered, but
they were nowhere to be seen.

CONCLUSION

As we are drawn into the Markan narrative, we warm more
and more to the little people. They, rather than the twelve,
exemplify the genuine values of the kingdom: trust and
self-giving service. Throughout the gospel they stand in
contrast to the religious authorities who are implacably
hostile and closed to Jesus. They recognise their need,
and come to Jesus in trust, openness and dependence,
sometimes overcoming serious obstacles. Thus, they
illustrate the fundamental gospel value of poverty of spirit.
They also come to experience the gracious acceptance of
Jesus, his freeing and healing touch, his saving love and
compassion.

---

14 The section from 8:31-10:45 is structured in such a way that there are three
   passion predictions, each followed by an indication of the disciples' failure
   to comprehend, and this in turn is followed by positive instruction from
   Jesus about discipleship, understood in terms of losing oneself, and service.
   The section is framed by the two stories in which a blind man is cured.

These little people also stand as foils to the disciples. Their willingness to forget themselves in the service of others, or in the service of Jesus, brings into higher relief the disciples' failure to understand, and make their own, the basic value of servanthood as, in their continuing blindness and pursuit of status and power, they continue to 'think as men think not as God thinks' (Mk 8:33).

In warming to the little people, we perhaps become more conscious of our lack of trust in the Lord, and of our reluctance to embrace and live servanthood. At the same time, we probably sense the attraction of their response to Jesus in its hope-filled simplicity and abandonment. We feel drawn and encouraged to come to know the Jesus who reached out to encounter them, and who seeks us in the same way, and to experience with them the gentle, but strong presence of his kingdom.

4 | ON SHEPHERDS AND SHEPHERDING

Scripture presents us with many images of God, and suggests many ways of deepening our understanding of God's saving love. In this chapter I propose to explore the implications of the scriptural image of the shepherd as a paradigm for Christian living and ministry. It has long been a favourite image for God, and is perhaps the best known and most universally loved symbol of the person and work of Jesus, the Christ. It is a motif which features prominently in the Old Testament and recurs in the Synoptics. The potential of this symbol is most comprehensively exploited by the fourth evangelist. It is important now to allow familiarity to defuse its far-reaching demands or muffle its radical challenge, no less valid, I believe, in our technological world of today.[1]

---

1   This chapter is a revision of an article, 'The Shepherd Image in the Scriptures: a Paradigm for Christian Ministry', published in *The Clergy Review*, vol LXXI, no 6, June 1986, pp. 197-206. I am grateful for permission to make use of this material.

SHEPHERDS AND SHEPHERDING IN THE OLD TESTAMENT AND SYNOPTICS

In Mark 6:6b ff. we find a description of the sending out of the disciples on mission. Having been instructed by Jesus, and been present at several of his mighty works, and also at his rejection by his townsfolk, they set out charged with authority to combat evil and to call for conversion (Mk 6:13). On their return they report to the Master all that they have taught and done.[2] With great sensitivity, Jesus perceives their need for a break and a rest, and invites them to come with him by boat to a quiet spot away from the crowds. However, the people guess their plan and thwart their attempt by reaching the intended destination before them.

> When he came ashore and saw a large crowd, his heart went out to them, because they were like sheep without a shepherd (6:34).

Jesus realises that their greatest need is for instruction and enlightenment, lest they go astray in blindness and confusion, and so his compassion moves him to teach them many things, or at considerable length.[3] Later in the day,

---

2 Mark describes the mission of Jesus under the double heading of preaching/ teaching and exorcising (which includes healing). He uses the same rubric when considering the mission of the disciples (here, and also at 3:13-15). Some consider the comment that the apostles reported to Jesus 'all that *they* had done and taught' (6:30) to be a hint of the theme of their failure which will be developed later in the narrative.

3 I have treated the theme of compassion more fully in *Come and See* pp. 15-34. In the doublet of this episode (Mk 8:1-10), the compassion of Jesus issues directly in his taking the initiative and supplying the four thousand with food in a similar way. It is interesting to note that in his version John brings out the significance of the multiplication of the loaves in the discourse which follows. In the earlier part of this discourse 'bread of life' is thought by many scholars to refer to revelation, teaching (Jn 6:22-50); whereas in the second section (6:51-58) it refers to eucharist.

he provides them with food by mulitplying the loaves and fish.

Matthew has a similar phrase:

> The sight of the crowds moved him to pity: they were like sheep without a shepherd, harassed and helpless (Mk 9:36).

Here, however, the context and response are different. Jesus is going the rounds of the towns and villages, teaching in the synagogues, announcing the good news of the kingdom, and curing all kinds of illness. His compassion prompts him, firstly, to urge his disciples to pray to the Father that he send labourers to harvest the heavy crop, and then, secondly, to associate others with him in ministering to the people's needs, as he calls the twelve, and sends them out with authority 'to drive out unclean spirits and to cure every kind of illness and infirmity' (Mk 10:1).

The description of the people in these texts as 'sheep without a shepherd' is found in several Old Testament locations. For instance, Moses pleads with Yahweh to appoint a leader for the community, 'to be at their head in all their undertakings, a man who will lead them out and bring them in, so that Yahweh's community will not be like sheep without a shepherd' (Num 27:17 NJB). As a result, Joshua is anointed and invested with authority. In 1 Kings 22:17 the prophet Micaiah, when consulted by King Ahab concerning the wisdom of proceeding to attack Ramoth in Gilead, is pressurised into disclosing his vision of the army in disarray: 'I saw all Israel scattered on the mountains like sheep without a shepherd' (cf. also Zech 10:2). Matthew refers to Jesus as having been sent to the lost sheep of the house of Israel (Mk 15:24), and as directing the disciples specifically to them when they go out on the mission referred to above (Mk 10:6). In his infancy narrative, in which many of the important themes of the gospel receive a first airing, he presents the role of Jesus, born in the city of the shepherd-king David, as 'a ruler to be the shepherd of my people Israel' (Mk 2:6, citing Mic 5:1).

The people of Israel were initially nomadic, and a strongly pastoral orientation continued. In Jesus' day there was still much sheep and goat farming. It is only to be expected, therefore, that the images of shepherd and flock should feature prominently in their literature.

In reading this literature we find that Yahweh is considered as the shepherd of Israel, though explicit references are rare. In blessing Joseph and his sons, Jacob speaks of the God 'who has been my shepherd all my life to this day' (Gen 48:15), and recalls that Joseph had been protected 'by the name of the Shepherd of Israel' (Gen 49:24). There are the opening verses of two psalms: 'The Lord is my shepherd' (Ps 23:1), and 'Hear us, Shepherd of Israel, leading Joseph like a flock' (Ps 80:1).

The people, on the other hand, are frequently referred to as sheep or flock:

> He led out his own people like sheep, and guided them
> like a flock in the wilderness (Pss 78:52; cf. 71:4; 79:13;
> 95:7; 100:3; Hos 4:16).

Many passages occur in which the shepherd role of Yahweh is strongly implied and vividly depicted:

> He makes me lie down in green pastures,
> he leads me to water where I may rest;
> he revives my spirit (Pss 23:2; cf. 28:9; 68:7; 77:20;
> 121:4).

The solicitous and protective aspects of God's relationship with Israel find moving expression through this imagery:

> Like a shepherd he will tend his flock and with his arm keep them together; he will carry the lambs in his bosom and lead the ewes to water (Is 40:11).

The returning exiles are described as sheep coming home to the evening fold (Is 49:9-10).[4]

Frequently in the Old Testmaent, Yahweh is thought of as delegating this shepherd-role to others. Some leaders, such as Moses, Joshua and David, fulfil their task well. Often, those to whom the flock has been entrusted prove unfaithful, and fulfil their responsibilities inadequately. This leads to situations in which the sheep are described as harassed and dejected. The wicked shepherds of Israel are trenchantly and vehemently upbraided by the prophets, notably Jeremiah and Ezekiel:

> 'Woe betide the shepherds who let the sheep of my flock scatter and be lost!' says the Lord (Jer 23:1).

These shepherds have fed themselves rather than their sheep, have failed to strengthen the weak, have not healed the sick nor bound up the crippled; they have not sought

4   See X. Leon-Dufour, *Dictionary of Biblical Theology* (London, Chapmans 1970), pp. 474-6; J. Jeremias in G. Kittel, *Theological Dictionary of the New Testament*, vol 6 (Grand Rapids, Eerdmans 1968), pp. 485-502.
The term is used of political and military leaders (cf. 1 Sam 21:8; 2 Sam 7:7; 1 Chron 17:6; Jer 2:8;3:15) and also of foreign rulers (cf. Jer 25:34-36; Is 44:28), but not explicitly of a reigning king of Israel, only of the Davidic monarch to come. Moses was accepted as a shepherd, and David exercised the profession for a time. 'Thus the figure of the shepherd was a noble symbol' (K.E. Bailey, *Poet and Peasant and Through Peasants' Eyes* (Grand Rapids, Eerdmans 1983), p. 147. However, in Jesus' day, shepherds were looked down upon. (See *ibid.*, p. 147; J. Jeremias, *The Parables of Jesus* (London, SCM 1972), p. 132.

the lost, nor brought back the strayed; they have ruled with force and harshness (Ezek 34:4; cf. Jer 2:8; 10:21; 12:10). As a result of such blatant lack of care, the sheep stray far and wide, a prey to wild animals.

So Yahweh pledges that he will himself go to their rescue, and seek out the lost, bind up the crippled, strengthen the weak, watch over the fat and strong, bring the strays back, and provide excellent pasture (Ezek 34:11-6). The Lord promises to give them shepherds after his own heart who will care for them, feed them with knowledge and understanding, and remove their fear and dismay (Jer 3:15; 23:4). Finally,

> I shall set over them one shepherd to take care of them, my servant David: he will care for them and be their shepherd (Ezek 34:23; cf. 34:30-31;37:24).

In responding to the needs of the crowds, who are harassed and helpless, by teaching, healing, feeding and sending others to minister to them, Jesus is considered as fulfilling these prophetic expectations. He is the awaited messianic shepherd.

The fourth evangelist takes up this insight and develops it, with considerable originality and depth.[5]

---

5 For the commentaries consulted in the study of this topic in John, I refer the reader to chapter 2, note 1; cf. also J. Beutler and R.T. Fortna (eds), *The Shepherd Discourse of John 10 and its Context* (Cambridge, CUP 1991).

THE SHEPHERD THEME IN
THE FOURTH GOSPEL

1. The shepherd in John 10

In order to appreciate the full import of the Johannine shepherd, it is essential to observe the context. The parable(s) and allegory of sheepgate and shepherd stand at the centre of a lengthy section which commences at the feast of Tabernacles (Jn 7:2), and ends with the decision that Jesus must die (Jn 11:53). Throughout this period the hostility of Jesus' opponents grows. There is a very close integration with the preceding incident, the magnificently constructed narrative of the man born blind, in which Jesus is presented as the light of the world (Jn 9:1-41). Towards the end is posed the question of the genuine leadership of Israel. For, the religious authorities, so full of their own importance, so self-assured and trapped in their legalistic parameters, have scorned the man and thrown him out of the synagogue, instead of welcoming him and rejoicing in his good fortune.

By contrast, Jesus has gone in search of him and led him to the insight of faith. The episode concludes with a confrontation and irrevocable division between Jesus, the light, and these Pharisees who, hardened in their blindness and sin, have forfeited the right to lead the people (Mk 9:39-41). There is no reference to a change in audience, no break in the narrative as we move into the shepherding imagery. The double Amen with which it is introduced does not normally indicate the inclusion of a fresh topic, but rather the expansion and elucidation of a theme already under discussion.

There are also close links with what follows. The attempts to stone Jesus (Jn 10:31) and later to arrest him

(Jn 10:39) are referred to in John 11:8-9, as the disciples
struggle to come to terms with Jesus' decision to go back
to Judea to be with the family of Lazarus. As a result
of the raising of his friend to life, the chief priests and
Pharisees call a meeting which is, in effect, the Johannine
equivalent of the trial of Jesus. There the decision is taken
that Jesus should die.

In the course of chapter 10 there are many allusions
to what is to follow.[6] It is against this background of
confrontation and under the shadow of this threat that
the theme of the shepherd is developed.

(a) Figurative discourse and the reaction: John 10:1-16

The setting is a sheepfold in the early morning. This
could consist of a square formed by stone walls on a
hillside or, as seems more likely here, a courtyard in front
of a house protected by a surrounding wall. It was not
uncommon for several small flocks to be jointly penned
at night, and often someone would be hired to watch them.
The fundamental issue, which ties in with the previous
incident, is that of the legitimate and illegitimate
shepherds. Two contrasts are drawn. Firstly, the man who
attempts to gain access to the fold by scaling the wall
is contrasted with the one who enters by the gate. The
former is classed as a thief and a robber, suggesting a

---

6   See U. Busse, 'Open Questions on John 10' in J. Beutler and R.T. Fortna
    (eds), *The Shepherd Discourse*, pp. 7-9. In the Synoptic trial scene (see Mk
    14:55-64), the accusations have to do with Jesus' identity as the Christ,
    the Son of the Blessed One, and with blasphemy. Both issues occur also
    in John: 10:24,33,36. For a discussion of this, see R.E. Brown, *New Testa-
    ment Essays* (New York, Paulist 1965), pp. 198-203.

stealthy and violent approach.[7] The true shepherd, to whom the sheep belong, is admitted openly by the gate-keeper.

The second area of contrast focuses on the different relationship which the shepherd and the stranger have to the sheep. On entering the fold the shepherd calls by name the sheep which he owns. It is not unusual for Palestinian shepherds to have nicknames for at least some of their sheep. Here the implication is that the shepherd has an affectionate name for each of them. They, for their part, recognise his voice and respond, and he assists their awkward exit. Once in the open the shepherd strikes out ahead, and the sheep fall in behind and follow. (The idea of the shepherd leading the sheep is a clear allusion to Num 27:17; Ps 77:52; Ezek 34:13.) The stranger, on the other hand, has no relationship with the sheep, so they do not recognise his voice, and refuse to follow him.

Those listening to Jesus fail to understand his figurative language. Given the events related in the previous chapter, such lack of comprehension comes as no surprise, for the Jews are blind to the light and deaf to Jesus' voice, unwilling to open themselves to the challenge of his works and words. In the synoptic tradition also, the general public, and even his disciples, cannot grasp the meaning of his parables, and Jesus needs to give explanations (cf. Mk 4:13 and 34). The clarification which Jesus now offers concentrates on the images of the gate (Jn 10:7-10) and of the shepherd (Jn 10:11-18). His explanation creates further division amongst his audience (Jn 10:19-21).

---

7   'Thief' is used of Judas in Jn 12:6; 'robber' of Barabbas in 18:40. It is a word which can designate bandit or messianic revolutionary.

(b) Twofold explanation and response: John 10:7-21

In verses 7-10 Jesus takes up the image of the gate or door
of the sheepfold, and claims that he alone is the gate.[8]
Others, be they messianic pretenders, priestly politicians
or religious leaders, he classes as thieves and robbers.
Their approches are illegitimate. There is only one door,
one source of revelation and salvation. The shepherding
of Jesus is unique and exclusive.[9]

The sheep who gain access to the fold through him
find safety and security; they have the freedom to come
and go at will, and are assured of pasture (cf. Ps 118:20,
and the synoptic sayings about entering the kingdom).
It is through Jesus, and through him alone, that the sheep
have access to the messianic community, and enjoy real
freedom and eschatological salvation, with its countless
blessings (cf. Ps 23:2; Is 49:9; Ezek 34:12-15). Once more,
with a further polemic thrust, Jesus contrasts himself with
the thief of verse 1, whose aim is to kill the sheep, and
as Satanic agent wreak ruin (cf. Jn 8:44), whereas the
purpose for which Jesus has come is to offer the sheep
rich, abundant and lasting life, life in all its fullness, the
life from above, the life of God (cf. 3:16-17).

In the second part of his explanation, the point of
identification switches from gate to shepherd (good, model,
ideal or noble), and the emphasis rests firmly on the
quality of his care for the flock. His goodness and dedication lead him to lay down his life on their behalf (cf. also

---

8   C.K. Barrett observes that 'John finds in the person of Jesus himself that
    which the Synoptists find in the Kingdom of God' (*John*, p. 307). For an
    excellent excursus on the 'I am' formulae, see R. Schnackenburg, *St John*,
    vol 2, p. 79-89.
9   See C.K. Barrett and R. Schnackenburg, *ad loc.*

Jn 13:37; 15:15), which far surpasses anything suggested in the Old Testament treatment of this motif. A shepherd's life did entail risk as is illustrated in the story of David in 1 Samuel 17:34. The joy amongst the shepherd's friends and neighbours in the parable of the lost sheep (Lk 15:4-7) is probably caused in part by his safe return. The same parable also hints at the suffering theme, not only in the fact that the shepherd's search entailed danger, fatigue and possibly pain, but particularly in what Bailey calls 'the burden of restoration', his being obliged to carry the sheep back to the fold on his shoulders.[10]

The good shepherd's generosity stands in stark contrast with the behaviour of the hireling. As soon as danger looms in the form of a predatory wolf, he takes to his heels and abandons the flock, which suffers harassment and is scattered. The shepherd's care stems from the fact that the sheep belong to him, whereas the hireling is concerned with his pocket and his skin, and has no personal interest in the sheep. Another differentiating factor is the mutual knowledge which exists between the sheep and himself: 'I know my own sheep and my sheep know me'. Such knowledge is not of the theoretical, intellectual type; as also in the Old Testament, it denotes intimacy, relationship, friendship-bonding. Once again the evangelist bursts out of the original framework of the parable(s), asserting that this relationship is patterned on, and results from, the relationship between the Father and Jesus. The implications of this statement are spelled out more fully in the discourses at the Supper.

---

10 See K.E.Bailey, *Poet and Peasant*, pp. 142-156; J. Jeremias, *Parables*, pp. 132-136; E. Linnemann, *Parables of Jesus — Introduction and Exposition* (London, SPCK 1966), pp. 65-73.

A new dimension is introduced when Jesus refers to other sheep of his which do not belong to the fold of Israel. These will listen to his voice; it is his task to lead them, too. A new flock, comprising both Jew and Greek, will then come into existence under the one shepherd. This will be brought about only as a result of his death and exaltation, for he 'would die for the nation, and not for the nation alone, but to gather together the scattered children of God' (Jn 11:52).

It is in the context of the Father's love, that love whereby God gave the son (Jn 3:16), that Jesus will freely fulfil the mandate which he has received, that he should lay down his life and take it up again. It is then that the fullness of life will become available and the new community will be created. Here again, we glimpse the depth of the shepherd's relationship with the Father, and his total orientation to the fulfilment of his mission, the Father's saving plan.[11]

The words of Jesus once more cause a split amongst his hearers. Many of them entertain the idea that he is mentally deranged, is possessed (virtually synonymous terms for the Jews of the day: cf. John 7:20; 8:48-52; Mark 3:21); listening to him is a waste of time and energy. Others, on the contrary, voice their reflection that his healing activity (specifically the miracle/sign in chapter 9), and the way he speaks, argue a power quite other than satanic.[12]

---

11 Whilst the rest of the New Testament views the resurrection as the action of the Father in raising Jesus, for John the Father and Son are so inseparably united that it is Jesus himself who takes up his life again, because such is the Father's will (see 20:5-7).
12 Other examples of division amongst Jesus' hearers are 6:59ff; 7:12-13; 7:29-31; 11:45-46.

(c) Dialogue at the Feast of Dedication: John 10:22-39

There is now a change of season. Several months later, Jesus is again (or still) in Jerusalem, walking in the temple precincts in the Portico of Solomon, which afforded protection from the cold easterly wind. It is the feast of Dedication, which commemorated the rededication of the Temple by Judas Maccabaeus after its desecration by the Syrians (cf. 1 Macc 1:54; 4:41-61; 2 Macc 6:1ff). The structure of this section is carefully arranged. After the scene has been set, the question of messiahship is raised and answered (Jn 23-30), and then that of Jesus' relationship to God (Jn 10:32-38). After each altercation there ensues a violent reaction (Jn 10:31,39). These questions have already been raised during the Tabernacles sequence (cf. Jn 7:25-31,40-42; 8:53f.); they are suggested again by the messianic implications of Jesus' self-identification as the shepherd.

With not a little frustration and hostility, the Jews at the outset challenge Jesus to make an open avowal of his messiahship, if that is indeed what he is claiming. In rejoinder, Jesus points to his works, done in his Father's name, which ought to have been sufficient to convince them (cf. Jn 5:36). He then takes up the shepherd/sheep imagery again. The fact that they do not believe what he has said, do not listen to his voice, nor accept the credentials of his works, indicates clearly that they are not sheep of his flock. The earlier explanations of the original parabolic speech concentrates on the gate and the shepherd; now the emphasis rests on the sheep. The sheep that belong to him do listen to his voice; they are known by him and they follow him. They receive from him the gift of eternal life and so will not perish. Their safety is secured, for they cannot be snatched from his care, protected as they are by one who is no hireling. Jesus adds that really it is the Father who has given him the sheep; the Father is the ultimate source of their safety and security. And he concludes with that astounding climactic statement:

'My Father and I are one' (Jn 10:30).

Whatever theologians have subsequently made of this assertion, developing its implications at the metaphysical level, it is in this context a statement of the evangelist's conviction that not only is Jesus the fulfilment of the promises and hopes concerning the messianic shepherd, but far more, namely, that the shepherding of Yahweh and of Jesus are one. In Jesus, the compassionate and solicitous love of Yahweh is enfleshed, is savingly present, offering life and communion.[13]

2. The commissioning of Peter: John 21:15-19

Just as Yahweh in the Old Testament delegated the shepherd role to others, so does the Johannine shepherd in the New. This takes place in the post-resurrection period, immediately after Jesus has appeared to Peter and his companions as they are fishing in the sea of Tiberias.[14] After the amazing catch Jesus provides them with

---

13 The theme of the shepherd is found also in the scene in the garden where Jesus allows himself to be arrested (18:1-11), and in the encounter between the Risen One and Magdalen (20:14-16). These will be considered in chapter 7. There is possibly a distant echo of the motif in Jesus' words to Pilate in 18:37: 'All who are not deaf to truth listen to my voice'.

14 Chapter 21 is usually considered to be an addition, probably written by an author other than the one responsible for the main body of the gospel, but like him a member of the Johannine group of disciples. He incorporates very ancient and valuable material, one form of the Galilee tradition of resurrection appearances.

a breakfast of fish and bread, prepared on a charcoal fire, a reminder of the charcoal fire in the courtyard of the denials. Attention is then focused on Jesus and Peter.

Jesus addresses Peter as 'Simon, son of John' as at their original opening encounter in John 1:42, after Andrew had introduced them, when Jesus changed his name to Cephas, the Rock. Three times he asks Peter whether he loves him. The first question includes a comparative, more than these (which is probably a reference to the other disciples rather than to his fishing tackle). Jesus does not countenance rivalry; friendship with him is not competitive; so the phrase is probably intended to remind Peter of his boasting that he was prepared even to lay down his life for his Master (Jn 13:17). The evangelist varies his verbs for love in the requests and replies. Some scholars have seen great significance in this; the majority, however, consider the variations to be purely stylistic and the verbs synonymous.[15] Peter does not take up the comparison; he is chastened by his recent experience. He simply acknowledges his love for Jesus. The third time Jesus poses the question, Peter's grief is evident; he is saddened and ashamed at Jesus' apparent doubt. Rather than boast, he simply entrusts himself to Jesus' knowledge of his heart: 'You know I love you'. Each time Jesus responds to Peter by telling him to feed his flock. Again, the evangelist uses synonymous words for variety and artistic effect.

We are meant to understand this episode firstly as Peter's rehabilitation. The threefold questioning and avowal of love are linked with the threefold denial. Jesus, the shepherd reaching out to his sheep, is affording Peter the

15 See particularly J. Marsh, *St John*, pp. 668-674.

opportunity of making up in some way for having let him
down so badly, assuring him of his generous forgiveness,
measured by the awesome responsibility he subsequently
bestows.

Secondly, the scene depicts Peter's pastoral commissioning. Some maintain that the threefold repetition of the
command to tend the lambs and sheep adds to the obvious
solemnity of the occasion. It is significant that Jesus insists
on love as a necessary prerequisite for this role, love for
him in the first place. Peter must be utterly devoted to
his Master; then can he be entrusted with the care of
the flock. The flock remains the flock of Jesus; the sheep
continue to belong to Jesus – my sheep. They are handed
into Peter's safe keeping. In the biblical tradition the role
of shepherd implies authority (cf. 1 Chron 19:6; 2 Sam
5:2). Peter shares in the authority of Jesus.

However, in delineating the characteristic traits of the
Good Shepherd, John omits all reference to power, status,
superiority, prerogatives. He emphasises aspects of pastoral
care: knowledge and familiarity, affectionate solicitude and
help, protection, and dedication. The outstanding note
of John's portrayal of the Good Shepherd is self-giving,
self-sacrifice. Our current text moves naturally to the same
theme, as Jesus indicates that Peter will also share his
destiny of violent death. During the dialogue at the
supper, Peter boasted that he was ready to lay down his
life for Jesus (Jn 13:36); subsequent events proved him
mistaken. Now the risen Lord assures him that he will
express his avowed love precisely in this way (cf. Jn 15:13):

> ... but when you are old you will stretch out your arms,
> and a stranger will bind you fast, and carry you where
> you have no wish to go (Jn 21:18).

Scholars dispute whether these words imply crucifixon specifically, or simply captivity as a prelude to death. For the evangelist, they clearly indicate that Peter will follow the shepherd pattern of Jesus and glorify God by obediently surrendering to death. Finally, Jesus adds the injunction: 'Follow me'. At the supper, when Peter asked where he was going, Jesus answered:

> 'I am going where you cannot follow me now, but one day you will' (Jn 13:36).

Now he can follow him, because he is no longer self-confident and is empowered from above. He can take the way of genuine discipleship which always calls for self-giving, and which, in his case, will demand martyrdom.

CHRISTIAN SHEPHERDING

It is not surprising that the early Christians soon extended the shepherd imagery to those with the charism of personal responsibility in the community (cf. Eph 4:11). In the Acts, Luke recounts how Paul, when en route for Jerusalem, summons the elders of the Ephesian Chuch to Miletus, and in the course of his address tells them to keep watch over the flock of which the Spirit has given them charge, 'as shepherds of the Church of the Lord' (Acts 20:28). The author of the first letter of Peter appeals to the elders of the community:

> Look after the flock of God whose shepherds you are; do it, not under compulsion, but willingly, as God would have it; not for gain, but out of sheer devotion; not lording it over your charges, but setting an example to the flock. So when the chief shepherd appears, you will receive glory, a crown that never fades (1 Pet 5:2-4).

Matthew's version of the parable of the lost sheep exhibits a similar preoccupation (Mt 18:12-14). Whereas in Luke, the parable forms part of Jesus' defence when criticised by the Pharisees for associating with sinners (Lk 15:1-7), in Matthew, it is located within a short discourse in which Jesus is addressing his disciples about relationships within the community. It is a call to the leaders to be persistent in searching for their erring brothers and sisters, for 'it is not your heavenly Father's will that one of these little ones should be lost' (Mt 18:14).[16]

CONCLUSION

The scriptural image of the shepherd is certainly a limpid window into the mystery of God and God's dealings with us, illustrating God's provident care and healing love. It is also a symbol which captures so expressively the reality and role of Jesus – his compassion, his teaching and revealing, his healing and solicitude, the life-giving and liberating intimacy of his relating, his faithful protecting, and his commitment to us to the extent of dying for us. It is an image which beckons us to reflection and contemplation, and to a response of trusting love.

This image also serves as a paradigm for Christian living and for the wide spectrum of Christian ministries: be that ministry lay or clerical, male or female, part-time or full, individual or team. Its implications for our being, our relating to others, and our reaching out in fulfilment of our mission, are spelled out clearly in the passages which we have considered.

16 See J. Jeremias, *Parables*, pp. 38-40.

We are called in our different ways and different contexts to teach and evangelise, to lead to enriched understanding; to heal and strengthen the weak, bind up the broken and crippled, feed and nourish, foster growth and fuller life. We are to know our sheep by name, guide them with gentleness, love them with compassion and deep affection. We are to create a space for freedom, a climate of trust, removing fear and dismay. We are to be prepared to search for and find the lost, and experience the joy and burden of restoration. We are to protect the sheep, being prepared to risk, to suffer, even to die. We are to shun harshness, tyranny, exploitation, self-interest, and avoid all forms of force and neglect. Shepherd is indeed a symbol explosive with challenge!

We also need to explore with courage and to discern with creativity what these pregnant phrases mean in the concrete situations of today's world and the contemporary Church. For instance, what kind of framework or ecclesial model can best foster mutual knowledge and affection, and create an atmosphere of trust and freedom? Who are the lost and the strayed in our context, and how do we reach out to them and offer them healing and pasture, and enable them to experience belonging?

As we look again at the background of John's presentation, we are obliged to acknowledge the cost of such love in our daily life and ministry, the demands and burden of restoration and service. It is also necessary to accept the probability of conflict and struggle and pain. Contrary to the indications of some forms of religious art, the shepherd image is far from romantic or comfortable. It is always overshadowed by the cross. The invitation to feed the sheep, to be a source of life, is by no means an offer of a sinecure.

The shepherd imagery calls us individually and collectively to examine and evalute the quality of our living, caring and ministering. We shall find that changes will be required, radical changes perhaps: changes in structures and pastoral strategy, and changes of approach, attitude and style in our relating. Such practical changes, however, will be unfruitful if they do not stem from a change of heart. The fourth evangelist indicates this by having Jesus preface his pastoral commissioning with the question: 'Do you love me?' Mission and ministry flow from relationship, action from contemplation.[17] We need to allow the Spirit to transform our hearts, fashioning and shaping them after the pattern of Jesus' shepherd heart. Our dispositions, values, outlook will then become more like his. As we grow to know more intimately his shepherding love for us and for all the sheep, we will be moved, motivated and empowered to continue his mission, and to do so according to his style, feeding the sheep in a manner which is a more faithful replica of his, and so we shall become signs and bearers of God's shepherding love to all whose lives we touch.

17 See J.D.G. Dunn, *Jesus and the Spirit* (London, SCM 1975), pp. 88-92.

5 | MEALS TOGETHER

Taking a meal, though the most normal of occurrences in our daily lives, can hold profound significance for all of us. It is an expression of friendship, at-homeness and esteem, and can be an occasion of great joy and celebration. Meals feature prominently in the ministry of Jesus. Amongst the evangelists it is Luke who develops this theme to the greatest effect.[1] He presents Jesus sharing meals with sinners, people on the fringe of society. Jesus dines also with the religious élite, whatever their motive for inviting him. Meals provide the topic for some of his parables. There is, of course, the Last Supper. Finally, the setting for the post-resurrection narratives is a meal. Through his treatment of the table companionship of

---

1   I am grateful to F.J. Moloney for this suggestion: *A Body Broken for a Broken People* (Melbourne, Collins Dove 1990), p. 59. His book has been useful throughout this chapter. See also J. Neyrey, *The Passion according to Luke* (New York, Paulist 1985), pp. 8-11; J.R. Donohue, *The Gospel in Parable* (Philadelphia, Fortress 1988), p. 140.

Jesus, Luke proclaims a message which is both comforting and challenging.[2]

JESUS SHARING TABLE WITH SINNERS

The first illustration of our theme occurs immediately after the calling of Levi (Lk 5:27-28). Here, Luke is following Mark. The story is linked with the preceding episode, the healing and forgiving of the paralytic.

Jesus sees Levi seated at his tax office and invites him to follow him, and thus break decisively with his normal way of life. His job probably entailed collecting the customs dues on goods arriving into the kingdom of Herod Antipas. Besides affording lucrative opportunities for extortion, which he seems to have benefited from, it necessitated frequent contact with Gentile merchants and officials. So the whole profession was stigmatised, and its participants were regarded as the dregs of Jewish society.

In order to mark the occasion of his entering into the following of Jesus, Levi holds a big reception for him in his house, inviting his colleagues and friends and many others with whom no respectable Jew would wish to

2   The following commentaries on Luke's Gospel have proved helpful: G.C. Caird, *St Luke* (London, Pelican 1963); E.E., Ellis, *The Gospel of Luke* (London, Oliphants 1974); C.F. Evans, *Saint Luke* (London, SCM 1990); J.A. Fitzmyer, *The Gospel according to Luke* (New York Doubleday, vol 1 1981, vol 2 1985); W.J. Harrington, *Gospel according to St Luke* (London, Chapman 1968); E. La Verdiere, *Luke* (Dublin, Veritas 1980); A.R.C. Leaney, *A Commentary on the Gospel according to St Luke* (London, A & C Black 1958); I.H. Marshall, *The Gospel of Luke* (Exeter, Paternoster 1978); G.H.P. Thompson, *The Gospel according to Luke* (Oxford, Clarendon 1972).

associate (Lk 5:29-32). They share table companionship with Jesus and he with them. The Pharisees and their scribes take umbrage at this disregard for the accepted standards and, presumably some time later, question Jesus' disciples about their eating and drinking with such appalling company. Jesus springs quickly to their defence and explains why it is that he welcomes sinners. He uses a medical proverb: people who are in good health do not require a doctor; it is the sick who experience such a need. A doctor's responsibility demands his presence with those who are suffering, not self-quarantined avoidance of possible contagion. Jesus asserts, not without a touch of irony, that his mission is concerned primarily not with those who consider themselves righteous, but with sinners, folk who are aware of their need for healing and forgiveness.

His table companionship is a gesture of solidarity, a healing and reconciling event; it is an invitation to receive the gift of repentance; it is a searching for real relationship, a breaching of barriers, an offer and experience of kingdom.

A similar situation occurring later in the ministry serves as the context for the parables of chapters 15 and 16. Luke writes:

> Another time, the tax-collectors and sinners were all crowding in to listen to him; and the Pharisees and scribes began murmuring their disapproval: 'This fellow,' they said, 'welcomes sinners and eats with them' (Lk 15:1-2).

Jesus seeks to explain and justify his attitude and conduct by recounting three parables, the parables of the lost sheep, the lost coin, and the lost sons (usually referred to as the 'prodigal'). The ministry of Jesus, the table companionship of Jesus, is about searching, like a shepherd in search of a sheep, a woman in search of her coin, a father in search of his sons, both lost in different ways. All three parables end on a note of celebration. The third parable is really the whole gospel in a nutshell, a magnificent revelation of God's compassionate love and purpose.[3] The setting of table companionship, therefore, is of enormous significance; it is itself a powerful parable of the kingdom; it, too, is the Good News in a nutshell.

The third episode introduces Zacchaeus, certainly one of the little people of the New Testament (Lk 19:2). Again, the context is important. The story follows the encounter of Jesus with the rich aristocrat, who was invited by him to sell his possessions and follow him, but proved unequal to the challenge (Lk 18:18-23), and the cure of blind Bartimaeus on the outskirts of Jericho, as the journey to Jerusalem draws to a close (Lk 18:35-43); it has a number of small details in common with each narrative. It, perhaps, served as a climax to that section of Luke's presentation of Jesus' ministry as the 'gospel of the outcast'.[4]

Zacchaeus is described as the 'superintendent of taxes', an unusual term probably indicating a responsibility for the collecting of customs dues on goods passing into Judaea from Peraea, and from further East. He has evidently benefited from the financial possibilities which such a post in the city like Jericho offered, for he is said to be extremely wealthy. However, he was eager to see what Jesus looked like, having heard, no doubt, of Jesus'

---

3   There is an absorbing and informative treatment of this parable in K.E. Bailey, *Poet & Peasant and Through Peasant Eyes* (Grand Rapids, Eerdmans 1983).

4   See J.A. Fitzmyer, *Luke*, p. 1218.

reputation in his treatment of people like him. His desire must have been more than mere Herodian curiosity. Caird speculates that it may have included a desire to escape from his self-imposed loneliness, the social ostracism which went with the job, to break free from a profession now burdening his conscience.[5] So he climbs up a sycamore fig tree to get a view, since his smallness of stature precludes that possibility amidst the crowd.

The spotlight now focuses on Jesus. It is he who, in response to Zacchaeus' interest, seizes the initiative. Jesus is aware of his presence, looks up at him, calls him by name, and invites himself to a meal and lodging in his home:

> 'Zacchaeus, be quick and come down, for I must stay at your house today' (Lk 19:5).

There is a note of urgency in his words. Zacchaeus is delighted. This is more than he has ever envisaged. So he climbs down with alacrity and welcomes Jesus gladly. He is obviously touched by the graciousness of Jesus, and his spontaneous offer of companionship, and all that this implies.

By contrast, the bystanders are scandalised by the fact that Jesus has chosen to be the guest of a sinner, and voice their disapproval. For, to their way of thinking, to share his table and home is to share his sin. Jesus frequently breaks through the barriers of religious prejudice with great freedom, and such freedom is a problem for others. As far as Zacchaeus is concerned, this freedom 'awakened to vibrant life impulses that had long lain dormant, and revealed to him the man he was capable

---

5   G.B. Caird, *St Luke*, p. 208.

of becoming'.[6] In response to Jesus' graciousness, and also to exonerate him from the crowd's suspicion, Zacchaeus declares that he turns his back decisively and without delay on his past:

> 'Here and now, sir, I give half my possessions to charity; and if I have defrauded anyone, I will repay him four times over' (Lk 19:8).

Without any prompting from Jesus, Zacchaeus implicitly acknowledges his guilt, professing his intention to offer alms beyond the normally expected twenty per cent, and to pay restitution far in excess of the legal prescription. This is a clear illustration of conversion, that change of heart and ways which is the genuine response to Jesus. Jesus is quick to recognise and affirm this in his concluding words.

Some scholars take a different meaning from Zacchaeus' words. Rather than a statement of what he intends to do for the future, they are an expression of his indignation at the crowd's assessment of him.

Whilst not denying that he is a sinner, he claims that he gives half his possessions to the poor, and that it is his custom to make reparation very generously for any extortion in which he may have become involved. 'He is an exemplary rich person who has understood something of Jesus' ministry, and message, and concern for the poor and the cheated.'[7]

The response of Jesus is addressed to both Zacchaeus and the crowd:

6   G.B. Caird, *St Luke*, p. 208.
7   J.A. Fitzmyer, *Luke*, p. 1220-22 and 1225.

'Today salvation has come to this house — for this man too is a son of Abraham. The Son of Man has come to seek and save what is lost' (Lk 19:9-10).

According to this alternative view, this is not a statement about forgiveness so much as his vindication of Zacchaeus' innocence despite his job. He is a genuine son of Abraham like any other Jew. And the gift of salvation has been extended to him, also.

Whichever interpretation is followed, and I incline towards the former and more traditional opinion, the last comment of Jesus sums up the scene, as it sums up his whole ministry. The language is that of the parables referred to earlier; it is the language and imagery of the shepherd. Table companionship is an initiative of saving search, a reaching out to the outcast, and it springs from his mission.

JESUS SHARING TABLE WITH THE PHARISEES

Jesus also shared meals with the religious élite. They too needed the Good News, and were not excluded. Luke records three such occasions.

The first (Lk 7:36-50) has similar features to John 12 and Mark 14, though it is probably a different incident.[8] It is preceded by the information that Jesus had a reputation for being a friend of tax-gatherers and sinners.

A Pharisee named Simon invites Jesus to dine with him. He obviously respects Jesus as a rabbi, a prophet even,

---

8 For a full discussion of this, see J.A. Fitzmyer, *Luke*, pp. 684-686; I.H. Marshall, *Luke*, pp. 304-307.

and perhaps finds aspects of his teaching attractive. His
welcome is polite but, as we learn later, lacks the gestures
which are special signs of warmth and hospitality. Having
left his sandals at the door, Jesus is reclining on a divan.
Usually the door was left open, and sometimes beggars
would come in to pick up the scraps, or admirers to relish
the conversation. On this occasion, the person who enters
is a woman who was living an immoral life in the town,
who had learned that Jesus was at table in the Pharisee's
house. Maybe there had been some direct contact
previously, or perhaps 'she had seen and heard him from
the fringe of the crowd, and that had been enough to
soften the hardness of her heart and to set her back on
the road to self-respect'.[9] Alternatively, she may have
been led to repentance and the beginning of a new life
through some indirect knowledge of Jesus and his
message.[10] We are not told. Her intention was probably
to use the perfume to anoint his head as a sign of gratitude,
but her emotions get the better of her and she breaks
down in floods of tears which wet Jesus' feet. Without
thinking, she lets down her hair, which is quite
unacceptable in public, to wipe his feet dry; she kisses
and anoints his feet. One can imagine Simon's
embarrassment!

'Through all this,' writes Caird, 'Jesus did not turn;
for he had no need; all that he needed to know about
the uninvited guest he could read in the mirror of Simon's
shocked face, and all he needed to do for the woman he
could do by accepting motionless the homage of her
penitent love.'[11] What Jesus in fact read was:

9   G.B. Caird, *St Luke*, p. 114.
10 See I.H. Marshall, *Luke*, p. 314.
11 G.B. Caird, *St Luke*, p. 114.

If this man were a real prophet, he would know who this woman is who is touching him, and what a bad character she is (Lk 7:39).

The words imply that he did not know, and that, had he been aware, he would have withdrawn from contact with her.

In fact, Jesus shows that he does know; she is a sinner, but a repentant and pardoned sinner. Then, through a parable about little and large debts freely cancelled, he brings out the significance of her actions and the contrasting dispositions of his host. He gently points out to Simon, not his lack of basic courtesy or failure to do what was necessary, but his economical love. There was no footbath, no kiss of friendship, no oil of respect. These the woman has substituted abundantly, effusively, with great love and unrestrained, spontaneous affection and gratitude, which reveal the pardon she has come to acknowledge.[12]

This is a moving narrative of two-way love. The woman shows so many signs of a love which is far from economical, and Jesus accepts her with great respect, allowing her to express her feelings, and even touch him. He welcomes the service she renders, and allows her to remain close to him, refusing to send her away even though the cultural and religious expectations warrant it, and even though the atmosphere is pulsating with shock and dis-

---

12 There is some discussion amongst scholars as to whether the sense of the text is that the woman's manifestation of love towards Jesus brings her forgiveness, or that her love is a consequence of her having been already forgiven, though this has not been recorded. The latter position, in which the parable is integrated into the narrative, is the view which I have followed. See J.A. Fitzmyer, *Luke*, pp. 686-687; C.F. Evans, *Saint Luke*, p. 362; I.H. Marshall, *Luke*, p. 313.

approval. Her love and faith are in such contrast with the cold, self-righteous, closed and withdrawn attitude of the male, religious élite.

The statement of Jesus: 'Your sins are forgiven', confirms what has taken place, assuring her of God's closeness to her through Jesus. The concluding comment draws together the motive which probably led the woman to seek forgiveness in the first place, her faith, her trust in God's openness to forgive, and two key aspects of Luke's understanding of what Jesus brings, namely, salvation and peace.[13]

> Your faith has saved you; go in peace (Lk 7:50).

On another occasion the Pharisee who had invited Jesus to a meal noticed with some surprise that he had not begun by washing which, though not demanded by the Law, seems to have been a Pharasaic regulation. Jesus reponded to the implied criticism with a strong attack on the kind of religion which is more concerned with external observance than inner conversion. It is not surprising that:

> After he had left the house, the scribes and Pharisees began to assail him fiercely and to ply him with a host of questions, laying snares to catch him with his own words (Lk 11:53-54).

The third occasion in Luke on which Jesus is said to have gone for a meal with a leading Pharisee, probably after the sabbath synagogue service, proves to be another flashpoint of controversy. We are informed at the outset that 'they were watching him closely' (Lk 14:1). Before him stands a man suffering from dropsy; it is not clear whether he is a 'plant' or a tolerated intruder, but his

---

13 See J.A. Fitzmyer, *Luke*, pp.687-688 and 692.

presence creates a tense situation. Jesus asks the lawyers whether it is permitted to cure people on the sabbath or not. They refuse to be drawn into offering an answer. Jesus goes ahead and cures the man and sends him away. He then presses home his initiative by questioning them about the legitimacy of what he has done:

> If one of you has a donkey or an ox that falls into a well, will you hesitate to pull it out on the sabbath day' (14:5 NEB).

If mercy can take precedence over law in the case of an animal, surely the same is the case when any human being is in question

This episode at the Pharisee's table provides an opportunity for the evangelist to bring together several sayings or mini-discourses of Jesus on the topic of meals, banquets or parties.

Firstly, observing the tendency of the guests to secure the best places for themselves, Jesus wisely reflects that rather than take a place near the head of the table and then suffer the humiliation of being asked to move lower in order to make way for someone else, it is better to take the lower place and allow the host to invite you higher. This saying goes more deeply than social etiquette, especially in Pharisee company, for the situation is paralleled in the spiritual realm also, in which 'everyone who exalts himself will be humbled, and whoever humbles himself will be exalted' (Lk 14:11).

Secondly, there is the topic of the guest list. Again, it is important to bear in mind the Pharisee context and their principle of refusing contact with those not of their kind, excluding from their table people who did not share their standards of piety. Jesus says:

> When you are having guests for lunch or supper, do
> not invite your friends, your brothers or other relations,
> or your rich neighbours; they will only ask you back
> again and so you will be repaid. But when you give a
> party, ask the poor, the crippled, the lame, and the blind.
> That is the way to find happiness, because they have
> no means of repaying you. You will be repaid on the
> day when the righteous rise from the dead (Lk 14:13-14).

Jesus is not against throwing a party for one's friends,
but he is emphasising the kingdom value of kindness and
hospitality extended to the needy and helpless, even the
unclean, those unable to do anything in return. Such openness, such lack of concern about recompense, follows the
pattern of God's gracious dealings with us in our poverty.
And it does, in fact, bring its own joyful recompense now,
and will be fully repaid beyond the grave.

The third discourse actually takes the form of a parable,
the parable of the supper (Lk 14:15-24).

PARABLES ABOUT MEALS

The context remains the meal in an atmosphere of conflict
in the Pharisee's house. The comment of one of the guests
provides the occasion: 'Happy are those who will sit at
the feast in the kingdom of God!' The focus of the parable
is not the group which makes excuses, but those who find
a place at the banquet, and in the kingdom.

A man was giving a dinner party and had issued many
invitations to his associates and peers. When the meal
was ready, he sent his servant, as was customary, to inform
his guests that all was now prepared. Although they had
previously accepted the invitation and were thus duty

bound to attend, they discovered more pressing needs which made it impossible for them to go. Such a refusal was a great discourtesy, an insulting affront. The excuses proffered had a hollow ring. It sounded like a concerted effort at rejection.

One claimed that he had to go and inspect a field which he had bought. In reality the inspection would have taken place prior to the contract and the purchase. The excuse is untruthful and insulting, implying also that the field is of greater importance than the relationship. A second felt obliged to go and try out his newly acquired oxen. This was a patent fabrication, as a price would not have been negotiated before the team had been thoroughly tried out. Again, there is the implication that animals have precedence over the relationship. A third stated that he had recently married, and did not even bother to excuse himself (cf. Deut 20:5-7).

On receiving news of these refusals, the host was understandably angry and insulted. However, he was determined that the banquet would go ahead without them. So he sent his servant to the streets and alleys of the town with instructions to bring in the poor, the crippled, the blind, and the lame. These guests probably symbolise the outcasts of Israel. Such a move was unexpected; it would also have infuriated the previously invited guests.

When this had been done, there was still some room, so the Master again sent out his servant beyond his town community on to the highway and along the hedgerows to compel them to come in. This suggests an invitation to the Gentiles, in accordance with the Lukan scheme of salvation history. The compelling motif is cultural. Unexpected invitations were also refused initially, especially if made by one of higher social rank. The invitation

would have to be pressed hard to convince of its genuineness. The offer is so unbelievably gracious. At the same
time, it stresses the urgency and seriousness of the invitation.

For the purpose of our theme it is the substitute guests
that are to be spotlighted. The invitation is consistent
with Jesus' opening declaration in the Nazareth synagogue
(Lk 4:6-30), which is taken up again in the beatitude of
Luke 6:20 and in the reply to John's disciples in Luke
7:22, that he has come to bring Good News to the poor,
the marginalised, the outsiders. It is in keeping with his
way of sharing table companionship. It is consistent with
his comment concerning the eschatological banquet in
Luke 13:29, that:

> From east and west, from north and south, people will
> come and take their places at the banquet in the kingdom
> of God. Yes, and some who are now last will be first,
> and some who are first will be last.

The religious leaders, who are closed to his insistent invitation and fail to recognise its crucial importance, run the
risk of missing out.[14]

There is another fascinating parable containing banquet
imagery:

> Be like people who wait for their master's return from
> a wedding party, ready to let him in the moment he
> arrives and knocks. Happy are those servants whom the
> master finds awake when he comes. Truly I tell you:

14 In my treatment of this parable I have relied heavily on K.E. Bailey, *Poet
    & Peasant*, pp. 88-113; see also B.B. Scott, *Hear then the Parable. A
    Commentary on the Parables of Jesus* (Minneapolis, Fortress 1989),
    pp. 163-174; and J.R. Donohoe, *The Gospel in Parable*, pp.140-146.

he will hitch up his robe, seat them at table, and come
and wait on them (Lk 12:36-37).

The context is a group of Jesus' sayings concerning the
need for the disciples to be prepared for the coming of
the Son of Man. They are to spend their time profitably
and be ready to serve him when he appears. The parable
envisages a situation in which the master is away at a
wedding celebration. The length of the festivities is
uncertain. The servants should be dressed for action, with
the long, loose-fitting outer garment tucked into the belt,
and with their lamps lighted, so that, when eventually
the master knocks, the servant can open the door with
lamp in hand to guide him out of the dark. The climax
of the parable is introduced by the typical emphatic
formula: 'Amen, I say to you', 'Truly I tell you'. Jesus
shocks his audience by a dramatic reversal of roles. In
that culture, it was unheard of for a master to wait on
his servants. Here, however, the master will fix his belt,
make *them* recline at table, and proceed to serve them
with a meal.

The saying of Jesus points to the Parousia. If Christian
disciples are willing to serve and wait patiently for the
final culmination of God's rule, they will find themselves
served by the One for whom they are waiting. But this
remarkable reversal of roles, utterly gracious, is not simply
a parousia promise; it is a reality present in the ministry
of Jesus, and is central to the great meal which is the
Last Supper.

THE LAST SUPPER

For Luke, the apostles share this final meal with their
Master as sinners and broken people, the last in that long

list of sinful people who have shared table companionship with Jesus during his ministry.[15]

After Jesus has told his gathered disciples of his longing
to share that final Passover with them, and after his words
of thanksgiving over the cup, he:

> took bread, and when he had given thanks, he broke
> it and gave it to them, saying, 'This is my body given
> for you; do this in remembrance of me'. He did the same
> with the cup after supper, and said, 'This cup is the
> new covenant in my blood poured out for you' (Lk
> 22:19-20).

He then breaks the dreadful news that one who has been
a frequent table companion, one whose hand at the
moment was on the same table of covenant friendship,
is his betrayer, one of the twelve. The others are taken
aback and ask among themselves: 'which of them it could
possibly be who was to do this' (Lk 22:23).

This leads into a jealous dispute as to which of them
should rank the highest. Perhaps this kind of conflict
concerning esteem and position arose on more than one
occasion (cf. Mk 10:35-45). The response of Jesus to this
outburst consists of a statement like that found in Mark,
and then a brief parable which is not in Mark:

> Among the Gentiles, kings lord it over their subjects;
> and those in authority are given the title benefactor. Not
> so with you: on the contrary, the greatest among you
> must bear themselves like the youngest, the ones who
> rule like ones who serve (Lk 22:25-26).

These are challenging and disturbing words for his
hearers, turning normal expectations, hopes, and practice

15 See F.J. Moloney, *A Body Broken*, p. 61.

upside down. Authority is to be shown in supplying the needs of the lowliest. Jesus presses his point with the parabolic saying:

> 'For who is greater – the one who sits at table or the servant who waits on him? Surely the one who sits at table. Yet I am among you like a servant' (Lk 22:27).

As in the parable which we considered previously, the reversal of cultural roles is quite striking. Jesus is indeed master; he is the Son, with a unique relationship with the Father and a unique role in the establishing of the kingdom. Yet, he is completely at home in the servant role. This idea is captured in the poetry of the letter to the Philippians, the famous hymn of 2:5-11:

> He was in the form of God; yet he laid no claim to equality with God, but made himself nothing, assuming the form of a slave.

It is dramatically portrayed in the footwashing of John 13:2-20. The parable describes the manner of Jesus' presence amongst them throughout his ministry, and provides the norm for his followers. Jesus is one who ministers to the needs of others. True greatness consists in a lifestyle of service and self-giving.

Subsequently, Jesus prays for Peter, that his faith may not fail, and urges him to strengthen his friends in their frailty. When Peter avows his readiness to go to prison and death with Jesus, the Master predicts his coming threefold denial. Jesus goes on to speak about the persecutions and difficulties which will face the disciples in their future mission, and they take his reference to a sword literally, indicating that they have two swords with them at the time. They have once again misunderstood. In deep disappointment, Jesus reacts by stating : 'Enough, enough!' – a reaction described by one scholar as 'the

utterance of a broken heart'.[16] Treachery, rivalry,
boasting, denial, complete misunderstanding, reveal the
disciples in all their inadequacy at this meal in which
Jesus' servant and self-giving love is so manifest. At the
end, he is obliged to face his destiny alone.

POST-RESURRECTION MEALS

In Luke's Gospel the meal theme does not end with the
supper. It is taken up again in the evangelist's telling of
the events of Easter day, the Emmaus story and the
subsequent appearance of the risen Lord to the gathered
disciples.

One very significant factor in the masterfully constructed Emmaus narrative (Lk 24:13-35) is that the two
disciples, who may well have been man and wife, are on
their way *from* Jerusalem. A salient characteristic of Luke's
presentation of the ministry of Jesus is his structural
emphasis on Jesus' journey up to Jerusalem. It is there
that the events of his death and resurrection take place.
It is there that the gift of the Spirit will be bestowed.
It is from that city that the apostles will set forth on
mission to the nations. Yet these disciples are walking
away; they have turned their backs. They are disillusioned
and disappointed; their hopes are in pieces, their expectations shredded. They have even heard the women's tale
of the empty tomb and angelic vision and Easter proclamation, but they are walking away in grief and unbelief.

---

16 T.W. Manson, *The Sayings of Jesus* (London, SCM 1971), p. 341. See also
J.A. Fitzmyer, *Luke*, pp. 1430-1431.

These are the two whom Jesus comes to encounter, with whom he walks, to whom he listens as they pour out their tragic tale, and whom he instructs on the meaning of it all, explaining the scriptures concerning himself, and the ineluctable pattern of suffering leading to glory. The miles have imperceptibly slipped by, and they find themselves on the outskirts of Emmaus village. Jesus makes as if to continue his journey, a gesture which provokes an offer of hospitality, genuine and open:

> Stay with us, for evening approaches, and the day is almost over (Lk 24:29).

Jesus accepts the invitation, and there is table companionship. Although he is the guest, Jesus acts as host, taking the bread, saying the blessing, breaking the bread and offering it to them.

> Then their eyes were opened, and they recognised him (Lk 24:31).

Again we find Jesus eating with broken people. He reaches out and touches them in their failure and disloyalty, their fragility and inadequacy, and breaks with them the bread of reconciliation. That outreach in table companionship transforms their understanding and reshapes their lives as, with a spring in their step and a smile in their eyes, they set out without delay to retrace their route and head back to Jerusalem, to share with the others their astounding and heartening news.

On their return these two disciples learn that the risen Lord has reached out to Simon in a similar way, extending to him, too, his enlivening forgiveness and companionship (Lk 24:34). As the whole company is gathered there together, excitedly talking about these extraordinary events, Jesus suddenly appears in their midst. They share a meal of fish together. Their companionship is re-established and renewed, a companionship which erupts into mission, as he sends them to proclaim to all nations the Good News of repentance and forgiveness (Lk 24:47). This Good News they have themselves experienced so profoundly in their table companionship with him.

CONCLUSION

The meal theme in Luke is wide-ranging and thought provoking. It can, I believe, be viewed in three perspectives.

Firstly, the Old Testament theme of the eschatological banquet, so strong in the prophetic writings, assumes a new dimension in the teaching of Jesus, as exemplified with stunning clarity in the parable of the great supper. The banquet gift is offered to all, beyond religious, and social, and national barriers.

Secondly, this eschatological banquet is anticipated in the meals of the earthly Jesus, his table companionship with the marginalised, the tax-gatherers, prostitutes, and sinners, the lame, the blind, the crippled. These are the poor who thus experience the Good News.

Thirdly, this anticipation is continued in the celebration by the Christian community of the Lord's Supper, the prolongation of the paschal experience, in which the risen one continues to be present in the proclaiming of the word and the breaking of bread.

In Luke's hands the meal theme becomes a powerful vehicle for the revelation of the significance of Jesus' ministry, his seeking and saving what is lost. Table companionship is a parable which epitomises the Good News: God's reaching out in compassion and acceptance. This message is addressed to us today. We are invited repeatedly to sit at the Lord's table in our brokenness, our weakness and fragility, and in our sinfulness. He is at home in our company. His presence assures us of acceptance and forgiveness and love and life. We belong with him. Perhaps we need to rediscover the wonder and mystery of it all.

As we look back to the meals of Jesus in remembrance, and look forward to the final banquet in anticipation, we are challenged as Christian communities in the present. When we celebrate Eucharist, it is important to recall that we are 'heirs of the poor, the lame, the maimed and the blind, physically powerless and socially shunned'.[17] Consequently, we must examine the quality of our hospitality and welcome, our openness to outsiders. For we have erected barriers, have developed attitudes and forms of exclusion, labelling people as sinners, differentiating between clean and unclean. Luke challenges us to reconsider our criteria concerning admission to the Lord's table, to re-examine more compassionately the difficult and perhaps ambiguous situations in which many of our sisters and brothers seek to work out their response to the Lord.[18] It is distressingly easy to lose touch with the mind and heart of Jesus.

Finally, the meal is a symbol, a catalyst, which presents a challenge to our daily living as disciples of Jesus. We are called to make our own, and extend to one another

17 J.R. Donahue, *The Gospel in Parable*, p. 146. This author's reflections are stimulating.
18 See F.J. Moloney, *A Body Broken*, pp. 130-137.

in the family and community, and to others more widely, the values expressed in Jesus' table companionship: genuine respect, acceptance, hospitality, non-judgmental forgiveness, presence with, solidarity, encouragement, compassion — a love which overcomes barriers and divisions. We are summoned also to creativity in finding ways of reaching out to today's marginalised, today's publicans and sinners, ways of communicating to them in our own brokenness the kingdom experience of table companionship.

6 | ON CALVARY'S HILL

For some time I have been interested in the ways in which the different evangelists describe the death of Jesus, the words they attribute to him, and the various phenomena which are said to occur. It is impossible and counter-productive to attempt to harmonise the accounts. One cannot but believe that the differences reflect the individual evangelist's theological and community interests. In this chapter I propose to examine the death of Jesus as recounted by Mark, and then John's version of the event.[1]

1 For the bibliography on Mark I refer the reader to chapter 3, footnote 4. Also F.J. Matera, *Passion Narratives and Gospel Theologies. Interpreting the Synoptics through their Passion Stories* (New York, Paulist 1986); G. Rossé, *The Cry of Jesus on the Cross. A Biblical and Theological Study* (New York, Paulist Press 1987); D. Senior, *The Passion of Jesus in the Gospel of Mark* (Wilmington, Glazier 1984); W.H. Kelber, *Mark's Story of Jesus* (Philadelphia, Fortress 1979). For the Johannine bibliography, see chapter 2, footnote 1, and I. de la Potterie, *The Hour of Jesus* (Slough, St Paul 1989); D. Senior, *The Passion of Jesus in the Gospel of John* (Collegeville, Liturgical Press 1991).

THE DEATH OF JESUS IN MARK (15:33-39)

Mark begins his presentation of the death of Jesus by referring to the darkness which covered the whole land for a period of three hours. This darkness is not to be understood as the description of a natural phenomenon, a sirocco or cloud formation; it is profoundly symbolic, and probably suggests the fulfilment of Amos 8:9:

> 'On that day', says the Lord God,
> 'I shall make the sun go down at noon
> and darken the earth in broad daylight.'

The long awaited day of Yahweh has now arrived. It is an event of universal import, of cosmic dimensions, and the end-time of salvation and of judgment, the turning point of history, the final battle between God and the forces of evil. The darkness of overarching evil seems now to be in the ascendancy.

The word of Jesus

> And at three Jesus cried aloud, 'Eloi, Eloi, lama sabachthani?' which means, 'My God, my God, why have you forsaken me?' (Mk 15:34).

This verse containing Mark's version of Jesus' last words, in which he is quoting the opening lines of Psalm 22, has proved extremely difficult to fathom.[2] Scholarship is divided as to its historicity. It is not impossible that in the crisis of death Jesus should have prayed the classic prayer of tormented Israel. This fact would also account for the importance of this psalm in the reflection of the

2   See D.E. Nineham, *St Mark*, pp. 427-429.

early Church, and for its influence in the narrating of
the passion. The early Church, it is maintained, would
hardly have created the tradition, for the words soon
proved an embarrassment, as their omission by Luke and
John illustrates.

Others believe that the tradition about the death of Jesus
included the element of a loud cry, and so the first
Christians provided content for that cry. The tradition
is certainly very ancient, as the preservation of the Aramaic
phrasing indicates. It probably goes back to the attempts
of the early Palestinian community to come to terms with
the cross, both for its own faith-understanding, and for
its kerygmatic outreach to Judaism. For the cross was
evidence not only of social stigma and shame, but also
of religious rejection. The cross stood for all to see as
the sign that the one who hung upon it was accursed,
and not of God (Deut 21:23). By inserting the opening
words of one of their favourite psalms, presenting Jesus
as the suffering just one, rejected, taunted, abandoned,
the community could place the death of Jesus within the
revealed plan of God.

The historical question remains open. The more urgent
issue for us is to determine what theological significance
the evangelist had in mind in accepting this tradition,
in handing on this cry as a vehicle for the interpreting
of the undisputed fact that Jesus died on the cross of
shame.

There are two main currents of opinion as to how the
cry is to be interpreted. The first places the verse in the
context of the whole psalm, which is a lamentation and
has two emphases. It stresses the pain and anguish of
the righteous one, his torment and abandonment, his
agony and death-scream:

My God, by day I cry to you, but there is no answer;
in the night I cry with no respite.
But I am a worm, not a man,
abused by everyone, scorned by the people.
All who see me jeer at me,
grimace at me, and wag their heads...
A herd of bulls surrounds me...
My strength drains away like water
and all my bones are racked.
My heart has turned to wax
and melts within me.
I am laid low in the dust of death...
(Ps 22:2,6,12,14,15).

The psalm concludes, however, as an expression of trust in the love and protection and faithfulness of God, the God in whom his ancestors had trusted and were delivered, and it shows unswerving confidence that God will vindicate him:

I shall declare your fame to my associates,
praising you in the midst of the assembly...
For he has not scorned him who is downtrodden,
nor shrunk in loathing from his plight,
nor hidden his face from him,
but has listened to his cry for help...
But I shall live for his sake;
my descendants will serve him.
The coming generation will be told of the Lord;
they will make known his righteous deeds,
declaring to a people yet unborn:
'The Lord has acted'
(Ps 22:22,24,30-31).

If the early Palestinian Church is responsible for placing this psalm on Jesus' lips, both aspects must be in mind, since its members looked on Jesus as the embodiment of the suffering just one tradition which, in the Sapiential literature, evolved into a theology of martyrdom. The just man does not seek to justify himself; he accepts his sufferings; he awaits God's vindication beyond the grave; and in this he proves that he is in fact chosen by God (cf. Wis 2-5).[3] Donald Senior believes that in the context of the theology of the suffering just one and Mark's Gospel as a whole, the words are unquestionably an expression of faith, not despair. Jesus affirms his unbroken trust in his Father, whilst feeling the full horror of approaching death. This, however, is in no way to downplay the dreadful reality of the experience of anguish and torment and abandonment.[4]

With sensitive insight one author comments as follows: 'The cry of Jesus summarises in an extraordinarily meaningful way both aspects of what is happening here: it is a radical expression of the loneliness of Jesus' suffering. He has to bear not only the experience of being abandoned by human beings, but also of being forsaken by God. At the same time, however, it is a radical expression of a devotion to God which endures in every adverse experience — a devotion which continues to claim God as "my" God and will not let him go although he can be experienced only as the absent one who has forsaken the petitioner'.[5]

The alternative line of interpretation is critical of those who invoke the whole psalm for seeming to dilute the element of anguish, for blunting its edge, for depriving the words of their profundity, and thus undermining

3   See G. Rossé, *The Cry of Jesus*, pp. 52-59.
4   See D. Senior, *The Passion in Mark*, pp. 123-124; F.J. Matera, *Passion Narratives and Gospel Theologies*, pp. 45-46.
5   E. Schweizer, *Mark*, p. 353.

Mark's intent. Taken at their face value the words convey dereliction, total desolation, an overwhelming sense of abandonment and, if authentic, plunge us into the supreme mystery of the passion.

This is the climax of the Markan theme of the isolation and rejection of Jesus. In the garden he was deserted by all his disciples without exception, including that youthful follower who narrowly evaded capture by leaving his garments behind (Mk 14:50-52). He was unanimously condemned as deserving of death by the Sanhedrin, the religious leaders of his people (Mk 14:64). He was denied and cursed by Peter, despite his earlier protestations of loyalty and love (Mk 14:66-72). He was disowned and rejected by his own people, who clamoured that he be committed to the hideous torture-death of crucifixion (Mk 15:13-15). The passers-by hurled abuse at him and mocked him in his helpless anguish. The robbers crucified with him joined in the taunting and renounced his companionship; he did not belong even with his fellow-sufferers (Mk 15:32). The prophet Elijah, popularly invoked as the helper of the just in their need, did not intervene to rescue him (Mk 15:35-36). The crescendo of loneliness and isolation reaches its climax in the experience of the absence of God. And it is only after the death of Jesus that mention is made of the women who 'were watching *from a distance*' (Mk 15:40). At the foot of the cross, in Mark, there was no mother, no beloved disciple; Jesus died utterly alone.

Some scholars, in the tradition of Luther and Calvin, believe that Jesus undergoes the punishment for our sins demanded and inflicted by the wrath of God. Others hold that he bears the burden of the world's sinfulness; he identifies with sinners, 'with everything there ever was, is or will be of sin-spawned alienation from God in this world'.[6] Paul speaks of his becoming a curse (cf. Gal 3:13), and of his being made sin (cf. 2 Cor 5:21). He experiences the full force of God's absence, penetrates the abyss of our lostness, plumbs the depths of our doubts, when all supports are taken away. Mark has Jesus die without any relieving feature at all, presenting us with a picture of Jesus as utterly desolate — draining the cup of suffering to the dregs... 'Jesus now experienced the bitterest blow which can befall the religious person — the sense of being let down by God'.[7] This seems to be the moment of defeat and utter powerlessness, revealing the vulnerability of love. There is something dreadfully stark and raw and brutally inglorious about Jesus' death.

Following G. Rossé I believe that elements of both these lines of interpretation coalesce in the total Markan perspective. It is inadequate to understand Psalm 22 in the Old Testament terms alone. From the opening of his Gospel, Mark has proclaimed Jesus as Son of God (cf. Mk 1:1). Throughout his ministry, his fundamental conviction and message is the gracious nearness of God's reign. In Gethsemane Jesus prays to God as Abba, a term which expresses deep intimacy and assurance (cf. Mk 14:36). It is for this God with whom he is uniquely bonded that he cries out; and this adds new profundity and poignancy to his sense of abandonment.

It is also necessary to recall that Mark has three times reported Jesus' prediction of his death and vindication (cf. Mk 8:31; 9:31; 10:32). There it is clear that Jesus

---

6   E. Schillebeekx, *Christ the Sacrament* (London, Sheed & Ward 1963), p. 31.
7   M.D. Hooker, *St Mark*, p. 375; see also her *The Message of Mark* (London, Epworth 1983), pp. 102-104.

saw his destiny in terms of the Father's will, and was
open to that will in surrender. This option receives
renewed emphasis in Gethsemane in the scene which
serves as a key for the correct understanding of the passion
narrative. There Jesus prays:

> Abba, Father, all things are possible to you; take this
> cup from me. Yet not my will but yours (Mk 14:36).

These words are like a shaft of light penetrating the
darkness. Behind the impression of total failure, at the
core of the experience of abandonment and absence, in
the focal point of human estrangement, and beyond the
brutality of the event, there unfolds a story of love. For
'Jesus loved in such a way as to experience separation,
disunity, abandonment: the loss of God for the love of
God... The extreme abandonment is in reality the fullness
of love, the profound loneliness is total unity. At the
moment in which he appears forsaken, he is identified
more than ever with the divine will; he is transparent
to the Father'.[8]

Subsequent events

In the immediate aftermath of Jesus' death are narrated
two events of considerable theological significance, which
bring out the effect and implications of what has taken
place. The first is that the curtain of the temple was torn
in two from top to bottom (Mk 15:38). There were in
fact two temple veils, one hanging at the entrance, the
other separating the Holy of Holies from the Holy Place,

---

8   G. Rossé, *The Cry of Jesus*, pp. 67-68; his exposé runs from pp. 60-71.

through which the High Priest alone was allowed to pass once a year. Mark is not specific. He probably intends a twofold meaning.

Firstly, the rending of the curtain symbolises the future destruction of the temple by the Romans, seen as God's judgment of the people for their rejection of their messiah. It also denotes the end of the temple cult and the Old Testament dispensation as a whole. The temple no longer has any significance. The action of Jesus in cleansing the temple (Mk 11:15-19), coupled with the incident of the barren fig tree which frames it, was a prophetic sign of coming judgment and destruction, a condemnation of corrupt and fruitless worship. Ironically, the words of those who falsely accused Jesus during the trial (Mk 14:57-58), and of the passers-by who mocked him on the cross (Mk 15:29), are brought to realisation, and a new temple not made by hands, the Christian community is about to come into existence.[9]

Secondly, the tearing of the temple veil symbolises the removal of the barrier between God and humankind; everyone now has access to a gracious God, the possibility of entering into a new relationship with God, including the Gentiles, as the following episode eloquently illustrates. These two meanings are not mutually exclusive, but are complementary: 'a curtain that is torn from top to bottom is at the same time an irremediable destruction and a decisive opening'.[10] The symbolism draws us back to the torn body of the crucified Jesus, emptied and seemingly destroyed, which becomes the new temple not

---

9 See D. Senior, *Mark*, pp. 126-128; and also M.D. Hooker, *The Message of Mark*, pp. 81-83.

10 P. Lamarche, quoted in G. Rossé, *The Cry of Jesus*, p. 20.

made by hands, the new sanctuary where we can encounter God (see Heb 10:20), the locus of the new covenant.

The second event consists in the response to what has occurred made by the centurion responsible for the execution:

> The centurion, who was standing in front of him, had seen how he had died, and he said, 'In truth this man was Son of God' (Mk 15:39 NJB).

Though the Greek text does not contain the definite article before Son, it is generally agreed that Mark intended the centurion's comment to be understood in this way. The gospel began with the presentation of Jesus as the Son of God (Mk 1:1), and he was proclaimed as such by the heavenly voice on the occasion of his baptism (Mk 1:11), and at the transfiguration (Mk 9:7). The evil spirits were quick to recognise this also (Mk 3:11; 5:7). However, this is the first time in the course of the gospel narrative that a human being has realised Jesus' true identity. The centurion's exclamation is an unqualified profession of his faith, and comes as the climax not only of the passion story, but of the whole gospel. It is also of significance for Mark that the first to recognise Jesus is a gentile. It is of crucial importance that he is brought to such an awareness through the *death* of Jesus. Neither the preaching nor the mighty works of Jesus has succeeded in penetrating the blindness and incomprehension of his disciples or the people. Jesus was condemned for blasphemy on the grounds of his messianic claim (Mk 14:62), and mocked on the cross as the messianic king of Israel (Mk 15:32). It is in that total losing of self in death, that complete self-gift in the service of others that his divine sonship and the nature of his messiahship — his deepest reality — are revealed and can be understood.

These two signs, thematically linked with the trial narrative, proclaim symbolically the reversal of the situation of failure, and are a prelude to resurrection, indicating that God is on the side of the abandoned one, and is powerfully present in absence. In his abandonment Jesus bears witness 'to his unity with the Father and to what the love of God is'.[11]

There is so much here upon which to reflect, about which to pray. We all know at first hand the meaning of loneliness in its various forms: the jarring sadness of bereavement, the corrosive listlessness of loss and separation, the alienation and shame of guilt and sin, the disappointment of failure, the isolation of intense physical suffering, the spent strength and seeming irrelevance of old age, the destructive discouragement and paralysis of non-acceptance and rejection, the pain of misunderstanding and estrangement, the gnawing emptiness of unfulfilled longing for intimacy and genuine companionship.[12]

There have been times for all of us, I am sure, when God has seemed very far away, times when we have been baffled and bewildered by God's ways. It will not be difficult for us to recall some of them. No doubt we have also been drawn into the pain and anguish and failure of others, and their sense of abandonment: as loved ones die, sometimes unexpectedly and suddenly, sometimes still young; as marriages break up and partners are deserted and children are caught in the middle ground; as businesses fail; as people are made redundant, and others

---

11 G. Rossé, *The Cry of Jesus*, p. 71.
12 See M.T. Winstanley, *Come and See*, pp. 108-110.

cannot find work and face despair; as young people fall victim to drug abuse and Aids... There are also the questions of our wider world amidst the ravages of natural disasters and those made by human beings: the tragedies of hunger, homelessness, civil strife and war, of appalling injustice, cruelty, exploitation and selfishness...

The cry of Jesus springs easily to our lips. We are drawn into the paradox and mystery of Calvary: that God was never so near as when God seemed furthest away.

As we struggle to understand, to see meaning, and to cope, we can, I believe, find strength in the knowledge that Jesus identified with our human suffering in its many dimensions, and most of all with our sense of the loss or absence of God. In his death and abandonment he was totally on the side of God and completely at one with us. As his disciples, we are invited to abandon ourselves in him to that faithful God in pain-filled trust, in openness to the God who makes the dead live and calls into being things that are not (cf. Rom 4:17).

THE DEATH OF JESUS IN JOHN (19:28-37)

John's presentation of the death of Jesus is so strikingly different from that of Mark. The atmosphere is one of majestic calm. Jesus is in complete control throughout, dictating the sequence of events and their termination. I would like to reflect with you on three themes: the word of accomplishment, the word of thirst, and the subsequent events.

The word of accomplishment

The last words which Jesus speaks on Calvary are: 'It is accomplished'. The Greek verb used here (*telein*) appears three times in the first three verses of this passage. It is one of those characteristic and particularly significant Johannine words. The hallmark of Jesus throughout the Fourth Gospel is his commitment to the fulfilling of the Father's will. His love of the Father finds expression in his surrender to mission.

> For me it is meat and drink to do the will of him who sent me until I have finished his work (Jn 4:34).

> The work my Father has given me to do and to finish, the very work I have in hand, testifies that the Father has sent me (Jn 5:36).

> I have come down from heaven, to do not my own will, but the will of him who sent me (Jn 6:38).

> ... but the world must be shown that I love the Father, and am doing what he commands; come, let us go! (Jn 14:31).

> I have glorified you on earth by finishing the work which you gave me to do (Jn 17:4).

For John, the pre-existent Word is turned in loving relationship to the Father (Jn 1:1), and the Word-become-flesh lives in total loving surrender to the Father in carrying out his task, that for which he is sent from above. The mission of Jesus, the purpose of his coming into the world, is to be the light of the world, the unique and authoritative revealer of the Father (Jn 8:2; 9:5), and to give life to the world, life in all its fullness (Jn 10:1).

The root word, which we are considering, is found also at the beginning of the Supper.

It was before the Passover festival, and Jesus knew that
his hour had come and that he must leave this world
and go to the Father. He had always loved his own who
were in the world, and he loved them to the end (Jn
13:1), [or] he was to show the full extent of his love (NEB).

The phrase *'eis telos'* is open to two meanings: it can have
a chronological connotation – the temporal ending,
simply; and it can also carry a qualitative significance
– to the full extent, completely. The evangelist has both
in mind here. The subsequent self-effacing and self-giving
act of service in washing his disciples' feet was a prophetic
gesture, indicating the import of what would shortly occur
on Calvary:

> There is no greater love than this, that someone should
> lay down one's life for one's friends (Jn 15:13).

So the last words of Jesus, whilst conveying the terrible
finality of death, are not a cry of dereliction, but a shout
of triumph. 'The revelation and the deed of love were
complete', as Barrett puts it so succinctly.[13] The limit of
love was reached, the goal of love attained. Jesus has
consciously brought to an end and totally fulfilled his
messianic mission in loving surrender.

The statement about the fulfilment of scripture in the
opening verse of our passage is usually interpreted as
pointing forward to the words: 'I thirst', and is thought
to contain a reference to Psalm 69:22: 'when I was thirsty
they gave me vinegar to drink' (cf. also Ps 22:16). The
Belgian scholar Ignace de la Potterie, however, is of the
opinion that it should be taken retrospectively. It is a
comment on all that has gone before, culminating in the

---

13 C.K. Barrett, *John*, p. 553.

scene which has just been described: the founding of the eschatological community, the Church, indicated in the words of Jesus to his mother and the beloved disciple standing beneath the cross (Jn 19:26-27). It should be rendered: 'After this, Jesus, knowing that all was now finished so that the scripture might be fulfilled, said: "I thirst"'. The phrase means that everything which has to do with his messianic task contained in scripture has now been fulfilled.[14]

I spent considerable time praying this 'It is finished' text in the final year of my mandate as Provincial, aware that the end of my term of office was fast approaching. At one level, naturally, I felt growing relief and great satisfaction in being able to say: 'It is (almost) finished'. But at another level I sensed a degree of near panic surfacing. 'No, I haven't finished.' There was so much which I had intended and hoped to do which still remained undone, and now might never get done. The form of service afforded by this particular ministry was slipping like sand from under my feet. Feelings of disappointment and discouragement washed over me as the catalogue of missed opportunities pummelled me, and a list of might-have-beens pounded in. If only I had shown greater confidence and courage, been more open and more compassionate and caring...

This wave of feeling generally ebbed away to be replaced by a growing desire to exploit to the full what still remained, and to strive to fulfil the Father's will more

14 See I. de la Potterie, *The Hour*, pp. 152-153 and 137. R.E. Brown, *John*, p. 908 suggests that the two possibilities should not be sharply separated. Barrett and Schnackenburg are amongst those following the more traditional position.

faithfully and generously. This experience, I realise,
mirrors so many other experiences in different situations
and at different stages of our life journey. The word of
Jesus can move us to thanksgiving and lead us into
repentance as we survey where we are and where we have
come from, and it can stimulate fresh effort and generosity,
can firm up our commitment and deepen our trust, as
we look to our future response to mission and to the
Father's will.

The word of thirst

That Jesus should have suffered terrible thirst is more
than probable. But John's motive for including this detail
is not simply factual; it is symbolic/theological/spiritual
– consistent with the tenor of his whole passion narrative.
Such thirst could express his longing to return to the
Father. Or it could be linked with the words Jesus uttered
at the end of the garden scene:

> That is the cup the Father has given me; shall I not
> drink it? (Jn 18:11).

In these terms he expressed again his surrender in love
to the Father, his commitment to the fulfilment of the
Father's will, his intention to drain the cup of suffering.
A view frequently proposed since the ninth century
maintains that Jesus' thirst may indicate his desire for our
salvation.

For I. de la Potterie, it is John's literary technique which
can indicate his true meaning. Firstly, there is the structure
of John 19:28-30, an alternating structure in which Jesus,
others and Jesus again are protagonists.

    Jesus: is aware that all is finished
             says: 'I thirst'
    Others: the vinegar incident
    Jesus: says: 'It is finished'
             handed over the Spirit

The two phrases containing 'finished' are in parallel, and 'I thirst' is in parallel with the handing over of the Spirit.

Secondly, there is what is called the misunderstanding technique, a device frequently used in this gospel. It consists of Jesus revealing a truth; this is misunderstood by his interlocutor(s); and the misunderstanding serves as a springboard for the explanation of the real revelation meaning of his words. A classic instance is to be found in the Nicodemus incident, when he takes Jesus' words about being born again literally, and Jesus proceeds to explain that he is not talking about physical rebirth, but about birth through water and the Spirit (Jn 3:1-10). In a similar manner the Samaritan woman thinks that Jesus' reference to living water indicates fresh spring water, whereas he is talking of water of quite a different order (Jn 4:10-15). In the passage under consideration, then, Jesus says 'I thirst'. The others, presumably the soldiers, misunderstand, and take his words literally, and soak a sponge in vinegar and hold it to his mouth. The real significance of his thirst, however, is revealed in his subsequent action of bowing his head and handing over the Spirit.[15]

There are two other important passages earlier in the gospel where thirst occurs. The first is the story of Jesus' encounter with the Samaritan woman mentioned above.

15 I. de la Potterie, *The Hour*, pp. 152-156.

Jesus and the disciples are travelling through Samaria and
reach the town of Sychar about noon. Jesus is weary after
the journey and sits down by the well, whilst the disciples
go off in search of food. When a woman comes to draw
water, Jesus says: 'Give me a drink'. As the narrative
cleverly unfolds, the perspective is reversed, and Jesus
exclaims:

> Everyone who drinks this water will be thirsty again;
> but whoever drinks the water that I shall give will never
> again be thirsty. The water that I shall give will be an
> inner spring, welling up and bringing eternal life (Jn
> 4:13-14).

From being the one expressing his thirst, Jesus is now
the provider of water to slake the thirst of others, living
water, which is generally understood to mean the revelation
and teaching which Jesus brings, and also the Holy Spirit,
explictly referred to (Jn 4:23-24).

The second episode takes place at the conclusion of
the celebration of the Feast of Tabernacles:

> On the last and greatest day of the festival Jesus stood
> and cried aloud: 'If anyone is thirsty let him come to
> me; whoever believes in me, let him drink'. As scripture
> says, 'Streams of living water shall flow out from within
> him'. He was speaking of the Spirit which believers in
> him would receive later; for the Spirit had not yet been
> given because Jesus had not yet been glorified (Jn
> 17:37-39).

The Tabernacles celebration in the Jerusalem temple had
a double focus. For seven days there was a ceremony of
light and a ceremony of water. On the eighth day these
ceremonies were discontinued, and the people rested and
rejoiced with music and prayer. On this day Jesus solemnly
announced in the temple setting that it is he who is the

light of the world (Jn 8:12; 9:5), and that it is he who
is the source of water. There is considerable scholarly
debate about the above text, and this is reflected in the
translation. One version reads: 'If anyone thirst, let him
come to me and drink. He who believes in me, as the
scripture has said, "Out of his heart shall flow rivers of
living water"'. Here the living water flows from the heart
of the *believer*. Whereas in the version which I am
following, the so-called christological interpretation, the
water flows from the heart of *Jesus*.

At Cana we saw that Jesus provides wine instead of
water; he is the new temple in John 2:13-22; he gives
new meaning to the sabbath in chapter 5; he provides
a new bread from heaven in chapter 6; and he will provide
new light in chapters 8 and 9. It is *he* who will be the
new source of water, similarly perfecting this aspect of
the old dispensation.[16] The new text contains three key
elements for our theme: the streams of living water from
within Jesus; the reference to the Spirit; and the orientation
of the fulfilment of Jesus' words in the hour of his
glorification, the hour of his being lifted up.

So the cry of the dying Jesus: 'I am thirsty', is best
understood, not without a touch of Johannine irony, as
an expression of his desire for the sending of the Spirit,
thus ushering in the new era, and completing his task.

Structurally, then, the thirst is parallel with the interesting phrase which John has invented to describe Jesus'

---

16 The former interpretation is followed by scholars such as C.K. Barrett,
R.H. Lightfoot and B. Lindars, and the RSV; the christological interpretation by R.Bultman, R.E. Brown, C.H. Dodd, R. Schnackenburg and the
NEB, JB, NJB. For a more complete discussion, see R.E. Brown, *John*,
pp. 320-324 and 327-329. See also J.W. Pyror, *John*, pp.39-40.

death: *'paredoken to pneuma'* ('he gave up his spirit' or
'handed over the Spirit'). Again, it is a phrase with two
levels of meaning. Clearly, it means that he breathed his
last, he breathed out his life, he died; and it conveys a
sense of serene and voluntary deliberateness. The evangelist, however, has already played on the multiple
meanings of the Greek and Hebrew word which can render
breath, wind, spirit in the scene describing the dialogue
between Jesus and Nicodemus (Jn 3:5-8). In the overall
context of the gospel, then, the deeper significance of the
phrase is that he handed over the Holy Spirit to his mother
and the beloved disciple in their symbolic role as
representative believers, thus inaugurating the era of the
Spirit, now that he has been glorified (Jn 7:39). John is
not saying that Jesus in fact bestowed the Holy Spirit
on Calvary. He later describes the risen Jesus breathing
on the disciples in the upper room on Easter day (Jn
20:22). John presents the several aspects of the hour of
Jesus in tight concentration: death, resurrection, ascension,
exaltation, giving of the Spirit. This Calvary outpouring
is proleptic, anticipatory, symbolic. It indicates the
meaning of his death, the ultimate purpose of his being
lifted up, of his returning to the Father.[17]

Dwelling on this word of Jesus: 'I am thirsty', I have
asked myself sometimes what it is for which I am really
thirsting, really longing. What is the nature of that deep,
troublesome, recurring thirst which I know is there and
which I often suppress or attempt to ignore or try to slake

---

17 See I. de la Potterie, *The Hour*, pp. 163-164; C.K. Barrett, *John*, p. 554;
R.E. Brown, *John*, p. 931; J.W. Pryor, *John*, p. 82. R. Schnackenburg, *St
John* vol 3, p. 285 rejects this interpretation, and D. Senior, *John*, p. 119
is of the opinion that 'it is more likely that the evangelist does not intend
to describe at this point the donation of the Spirit'.

with waters which will not satisfy? Like Jesus, I am aware
of a thirst to give: to give affection and support, affirmation
and encouragement; and to give something of what I have
come to know and experience in my life of discipleship,
for all its limitations; to share what I have been given.
I admit that I have not allowed this thirst to grip me to
the point of crying out! I am also aware of a thirst to
receive: to receive human acceptance and love and
friendship; to receive the gift of God's closeness and love
and fuller life; to be in the Father's presence. Thirst speaks
of longing and dryness and need. I believe that it can
be very fruitful to explore in prayer the range of one's
thirsts.

Subsequent events

After the death of Jesus, the fourth evangelist adds some
details which can be viewed as a theological interpretation
of what has taken place (Jn 19:31-37). The structure is
again interesting:

   (a) two events:
         one negative: they do not break his legs
         one positive: the lance thrust;
   (b) an emphatic centrepiece concerning the disciple's
       witness;
   (c) the interpretation of the two events through
       scripture:
         one negative: no broken bones
         one positive: looking on the one pierced

   The first event and quotation 'no bone of his shall be
broken' (Ex 12:46) reintroduces the Passover theme. The
element of haste points in the same direction. We recall

that at the beginning of the gospel the Baptist indicates
Jesus to two of his disciples as 'the Lamb of God who
takes away the sin of the world' (Jn 1:29). It is also of
interest that according to John's passion chronology, which
differs from that of the Synoptists, Jesus was sentenced
to death at the very time when the paschal lambs were
being sacrificed in the temple. Perhaps, too, the immediate
bloodflow suggests that Jesus died as a sacrificial victim
since, according to Jewish Law, the blood of the sacrificed animal should flow immediately at the moment of
death.

Incidentally, there is a subtle hint of this theme slightly
earlier in the Calvary narrative when the soldiers respond
to Jesus' cry of thirst by placing the wine-soaked sponge
on hyssop. Hyssop is a small bushy plant which lacks
the firmness required for this purpose. In the time of the
Exodus, hyssop was used to sprinkle the doorposts and
lintel with the blood of the paschal lamb (Ex 12:22-23;
cf. Heb 9:18-20). John's fertile imagination grasped the
symbolic potential and made this connection.

It seems, then, that Jesus is presented as the Passover
Lamb, slaughtered for the deliverance of his people; he
is the Paschal Lamb of the new covenant.

The second event is the lance thrust and the subsequent flow of blood and water, an item which is clearly
of major significance to John. At the factual level various
theories have been offered to explain the phenomenon
medically; it seems quite plausible physiologically.[18] The
detail, which shows that Jesus was well and truly dead,

18 For a survey of these views, see R.E. Brown, *John*, pp. 946-948.

would also have apologetic value against those who sought to explain away the resurrection. Once again, however, John's purpose is far more profound.

The flow of water, in the context of the gospel as a whole, and of the crucifixion scene in particular, must be a symbol of the Spirit. There is a line of continuity between the thirst of Jesus whilst alive (Jn 19:28), the gift of the Spirit at his death (Jn 19:30), and the living water pouring forth from within him which becomes the symbol of this Spirit-gift after his death (Jn 9:35). The incident recalls the water gushing from the rock in Exodus (17:6; Num 20:11), and the vision of the waters flowing from the temple in Ezekiel (47:1-12). It forms the climax of the theme of water which has coursed through the gospel narrative (Jn 1:33; 3:5; 4:14; 7:38f.; 13:5), and is in particular the fulfilment of Jesus' words in John 7:37-39. The life-giving Spirit flows out from the open side of the uplifted Jesus.

Analogously, a christological theme is expressed through the blood. There is also a line of continuity between the two expressions denoting accomplishment (Jn 19:28,30) and the flow of blood. The blood gushing forth is a sign that Jesus is dead. It also symbolises his life before death, his life which culminates in death. It is the symbolic expression of all that is meant by his words: 'It is accomplished!'; that loving, self-giving and serving which was his style of life and ministry; his obedience to the Father's will; his love to the end and to the maximum. We can thus penetrate the heart of Jesus.[19] The blood is the sign of Jesus' saving death (cf. 1 Jn 1:7; 5:6-8).

19 See I. de la Potterie, *The Hour*, pp. 172-174.

What was opened in death becomes a source of life. The living water of the Spirit draws us into the life of Jesus (his blood). We can share his life in all its mysterious depth, eternal life as the evangelist calls it. C.K. Barrett comments that 'from the Crucified there proceed those living streams by which people are quickened and the Church lives.[20] The mother of Jesus and the beloved disciple, present at the hour, represent the nascent Church. We, today, follow the Johannine community in being caught up in this life through the gift of the Spirit in the waters of baptism, and sustained through the sacrament of the eucharist.[21]

The scriptural quotation which accompanies the event of the lance thrust and the flow of blood and water concludes the Calvary scene:

They shall look on him whom they pierced (Jn 19:37).

It is taken from Zechariah 12:10. In passing, it is interesting to note what a rich source of imagery about Jesus is to be found in chapters 9-14 of that prophet. There is the shepherd theme (10:2-3; 11:4-17; 13:7); the king riding on a donkey (9:9); the thirty pieces of silver (11:12); and the feast of tabernacles and the living water (ch 14), which is part of the background of John 7:37-39. In the present context John does not specify who they might

---

20 C.K. Barrett, *John*, p.557.
21 The question of sacraments in the fourth gospel is complex, but most commentators would consider it probable that there is a secondary or less immediate reference here to baptism in the symbolism of the water, and to eucharist in the symbolism of the blood, clearer for baptism than for eucharist. See R.E. Brown, *John*, pp.951-952; F.J. Moloney, 'When is John Talking about Sacraments?', *Australian Biblical Review* 30 (1982), pp.10-33; D. Senior, *John*, p.127. J.W. Pryor, *John*, p.83, is of the opinion that no such sacramental symbolism is intended here.

be, nor whether they look in rejection, remorse or acceptance. The wider context of Zechariah is illuminating.

> On that day ... I shall pour a spirit of pity and compassion on the house of David and the inhabitants of Jerusalem. Then they will look on me, on him whom they have pierced, and will lament over him as over an only child, and will grieve for him bitterly as for a firstborn son... (Zech 12:10).

> On that day a fountain will be opened for the line of David and for the inhabitants of Jerusalem, to remove their sin and impurity (Zech 13:1).

> On that day, whether in summer or in winter, running water will issue from Jerusalem, half flowing to the eastern sea and half to the western sea. The Lord will become king over all the earth; on that day he will be the only Lord and his name the only name (Zech 14:8).

It would appear that John's idea is that the uplifted Jesus is the focal point of judgment, a theme which recurs throughout the gospel. At the cross are those who have rejected him and turned away from the light, and those who have accepted him (represented by his mother and the beloved disciple), those for whom he is, like the uplifted serpent in the desert, a source of life and salvation (Jn 3:14).

The emphasis in Zechariah is on conversion and hope. In John, too, it is salvation which is the dominant motif, for one cannot look on the pierced Jesus without seeing the flowing blood and water, which are sources of life. The uplifted Son of Man, the enthroned king, is the source of eternal life for the believer (Jn 3:14-15). His true identity and role will be revealed through his being lifted up (Jn

8:28). And when lifted up from the earth, he will draw all to himself (Jn 12:32). And the grain of wheat will yield a rich harvest (Jn 12:24).[22]

As Christian believers, we are invited to stand at the foot of the cross on Calvary's hill, aware of our sinfulness and need, and to gaze on the one whose side has been pierced. We gaze in trust and confidence. We look in faith, with the contemplative eye which discerns to some extent the significance of what we see, and in wonder and gratitude we open our hearts to the gift of the Spirit. We are humbly and joyfully aware that through that gift outpoured we are drawn into the mystery of God's life and love, as it was for this that Jesus was sent from above (Jn 3:16-17), and for this that he returned to the Father's side (Jn 13:1; 16:28). Through this gift we are also drawn into Jesus' community and into discipleship; we are made one with him. This entails our living according to his life-style of obedient self-surrender to the Father, and loving service towards others, which are symbolised by the flowing blood. Perhaps we shall linger long on this hill, as the implications of what we witness permeate our being.

---

22 See R.E. Brown, *John*, pp. 953-956; R. Schnackenburg, *St John*, vol 3, pp. 292-294.

7 | JERUSALEM GARDENS

Since my childhood I have been interested in gardens, and with the passing of the years that interest has increased. I am frequently moved to joyful wonder at the immense variety of shape and scent, the limitless rainbow of hue, blazing colours or delicately refined tints, and at the enormous range of possibilities in the harmony of tree and bush, shrub and flower and lawn.

Gardens are to me a constant reminder of the rhythmic mystery of life and growth which issues in death, death which births new life. Perhaps I was thus predisposed to find fascinating the way in which the gardens of Jerusalem feature in the Johannine version of the events of Jesus' hour.

There are two gardens in question: the garden in which Jesus allows himself to be taken prisoner by his enemies (Jn 18:1-12), and the garden in which he is later buried by his friends (Jn 19:38-42). These two gardens constitute the framework for the passion narrative. The second garden subsequently becomes the setting for the revelation which is Easter (Jn 20:1-18).[1]

THE GARDEN OF CONFRONTATION

There is a garden situated across the winter-flowing Kedron wadi, an olive grove facing the Temple mount resplendent in white and gold. It is a place which Jesus and his disciples frequently visited when in the city. After the final supper with his own, Jesus led his little flock there once more. In the course of that meal, he had said to them:

> I warn you, the hour is coming, has indeed already come, when you are to be scattered, each to his home, leaving me alone (Jn 16:32).

These words echo the Synoptic tradition in which, as Jesus and the disciples are en route for Gethsemane after singing the Passover hymn, he cites Zechariah 13:7:

> You will all lose faith;. for it is written: 'I will strike the shepherd and the sheep will be scattered' (Mk 14:27).

In Mark these words are quickly fulfilled, for at Jesus' arrest all the disciples take to flight and desert him. John handles the tradition of the arrest of Jesus and the flight of the disciples very differently, exhibiting great dramatic skill and theological acumen.

In his final prayer to the Father, Jesus intercedes with his own:

---

1   The reader is again referred to the Johannine bibliography found in chapter 2, note 1. In addition, see I. de la Potterie, *The Hour of Jesus*, pp. 45-61; D. Senior, *The Passion of Jesus in the Gospel of John* (Collegeville, The Liturgical Press 1991), pp. 46-55 and 129-133.

> Holy Father, protect them by the power of your name,
> the name you have given me, that they may be one, as
> we are one. While I was with them, I protected them
> by the power of your name which you gave me, and
> kept them safe (Jn 17:11-12).

His petition evokes the shepherd imagery of John 10,
which we considered in an earlier chapter. In the face
of the hostile party which comes out to arrest him, the
protective care of Jesus for his flock is exemplified. The
scene is the good shepherd parable in action.[2]

It is black night when Judas, painfully designated as
the traitor (cf. Jn 6:64,72; 13:2,11,21), in whom Satan has
already entered (Jn 13:27), reaches the place, bringing with
him the Jewish police sent by the chief priests and the
Pharisees (cf. also Jn 7:32,45; 11:47,57), and the Gentile
soldiery, heavily armed with swords and clubs, strangely
at one in their destructive quest for the man from
Nazareth.[3] They carry lanterns and brightly burning
torches for this confrontation between the powers of
darkness and the light of the world! Dramatic confrontation it is, as representatives of the Jewish and Gentile
worlds, the secular and religious powers, with Judas
standing in their midst, are arrayed against Jesus. The
final struggle between good and evil is about to be joined.

Jesus, his hour now come, and firmly embraced, takes
the initiative and moves forward to meet them, thus

2 In John's Gospel there is no agony scene between the supper and Jesus'
   arrest. Key elements are found, however, in 12:27-28.
3 The presence of Roman soldiers in the arresting party is not entirely
   implausible historically; cf. R.E. Brown, *John*, pp. 807-808 and 814-817;
   D. Senior, *John*, pp. 49-50. R. Schnackenburg, however, thinks it 'as good
   as impossible' (*St John*, vol 3, p. 222). Whatever the historical considerations, the evangelist certainly intended his readers to understand the
   detachment as Roman.

obviating the need for the identifying kiss. He asks whom
they are looking for, a question once asked of the first
disciples (Jn 1:38) and to be asked again in our second
garden (Jn 20:15). On being informed that they seek Jesus
of Nazareth, he majestically exclaimed: 'I am he'. At this,
they all draw back and fall to the ground. His reply means
more than simply: 'I am the man you are looking for'.
According to many scholars it has a double significance,
and is to be interpreted also along the lines of the other
'I am' sayings in John. Jesus applies to himself the divine
name revealed in the Old Testament, a name expressing
the holiness and transcendence of God (cf. Is 43:10). The
reaction confirms this. The police and soldiers are stricken
with awe and rendered utterly powerless when confronted
with the might of God in Jesus (cf. 2 Kings 1:9-14; Is
11:4; Ps 56:9; 27:2; 10:4; Dan 2:46; 8:18). The fourth
evangelist makes it clear that Jesus is entirely in control
of the situation. His life will not be taken from him. He
lays it down freely in surrender to the Father's will, as
he has already explicitly indicated (Jn 10:18).

Jesus reiterates his question, and they their answer. This
time he continues:

> I have told you that I am he. If I am the man you want,
> let these others go (Jn 18:8).

The narrator here reminds us that; 'this was to make good
his words, "I have not lost one of those you gave me"'
(cf. Jn 10:27-28; 6:39; 17:12). In this way Jesus obtains
for the disciples the freedom to leave honourably without
molestation. The episode is an illustration of the shepherd's willing acceptance of suffering and death so that
the sheep may have life.

Simon Peter, in impetuous violence, unsheathes his
sword and cuts off the ear of the high priest's servant,

Malchus. It is an act which totally misreads the situation, for Jesus freely accepts to drink the cup which his Father has given him. This is the reason for which he has come to this hour (Jn 12:27). He allows himself to be taken and bound, so that he may be lifted up to reveal the saving love of God.

THE GARDEN OF BURIAL

The other garden is situated conveniently near the Place of the Skull, where the crucifixion and death of Jesus have taken place. Joseph of Arimathaea, probably a member of the Sanhedrin (Mk 15:43 and Lk 23:50), having courageously sought and obtained Pilate's permission to remove Jesus' body from the cross, brings it for burial. The evangelist describes Joseph as a disciple of Jesus, who has kept his allegiance secret for fear of the Jews. In John 12:42 we read:

> For all that, even among those in authority many believed in him, but would not acknowledge him on account of the Pharisees, for fear of being banned from the synagogue. For they valued human reputation rather than the honour which comes from God.

He now sheds his fear and inhibitions and publicly sets about providing Jesus with a decent and honourable burial, thus expressing unequivocally his commitment and devotion.

In this he is joined by Nicodemus, who was introduced earlier in the narrative as 'one of the Pharisees, a leader of the Jews' (Jn 3:1). John reminds us that he has first approached Jesus by night, probably also through fear.

Already at that stage he was open to Jesus, beginning to
emerge from the dark into the light:

> Rabbi, we know that you are a teacher sent by God;
> no one could perform these signs of yours unless God
> were with him (Jn 3:2).

Later in the narrative, when, during the celebration of
Tabernacles, the police return to the Pharisees empty
handed after an abortive attempt to apprehend Jesus, and
receive for their pains a vehement tirade of disapproval,
Nicodemus takes the risk of breaking cover and comes
to Jesus' defence by reminding his peers that according
to the Law they should not pass judgment on Jesus
without giving him a hearing and discovering what he
is about. For this he incurs their wrath and sarcasm (Jn
7:45-52). Evidently, there remains some hesitancy and
ambiguity in his response to Jesus.

Now he joins Joseph in coming out into the light and
showing his true colours. Both throw aside their fears
and openly acknowledge their allegiance and affection.
The words of Jesus are now coming true:

> And when I am lifted up from the earth I shall draw
> everyone to myself (Jn 12:32).

New life and light are flowing from the pierced side of
the uplifted Jesus.[4]

Drawn together in open discipleship, the two men set
about the burial of Jesus. Nicodemus has brought with

---

4   There is a strong ecclesiological aspect to the Johannine passion narrative.
     The crucifixion scene is understood as the kingly Jesus founding the Church
     and pouring down his Spirit upon it. Joseph and Nicodemus are now being
     gathered into the new community, the new People of God. Brown, *John*,
     p. 959, refers to the possibility that the evangelist is here also appealing
     to Christian believers who still frequent the synagogue to profess their faith
     openly, even though that will inevitably entail their excommunication.

him an enormous quantity of spices, more than a hundred pounds of myrrh and aloes. In the Synoptic tradition the body of Jesus is not anointed before burial. The purpose of the women's coming to the tomb after the sabbath includes the performance of this duty. Such a motive is precluded by John's presentation of the event. There is no mention of the women at all. The cloths are generously sprinkled with spices, and the body is lavishly anointed.

Whatever the historical details might be, John has a theological motif in mind, the theme of the kingship of Jesus.[5] The coming of God's Kingdom is the heart of the message of Jesus in the Synoptics, whereas in John it is mentioned only in 3:3, in the opening part of Jesus' meeting with Nicodemus. However, the kingship of Jesus is central to John's treatment of the passion. It is the accusation about which Pilate questions Jesus at the trial, which leads into Jesus' explanation of his understanding of the term (Jn 18:34-38); Jesus is crowned and mocked by the soldiery as king of the Jews (Jn 19:1-3); he is presented to the people wearing the crown and purple robe of kingship (Jn 19:5); his claim to kingship is rejected by the people (Jn 18:40; 19:15-16); and the notice fixed on his cross, in the three principal languages, is 'King of the Jews' (Jn 19:19-20). For John the cross is the throne from which Jesus the king reigns. Now, finally, the king is given a royal burial, for which no expense is spared, in a tomb newly hewn from the rock. The garden setting, too, may point to this interpretation, for the kings of Judah were buried in a garden (cf. 2 Kings 21:18,26; Neh 3:16).In this way, the Johannine passion narrative is brought to

---

5   For a comparison of the different versions and a survey of views, see R.E. Brown, *John*, pp.956-958.

a triumphant conclusion, and already the death of Jesus has begun to bring about a transformation.

These two garden narratives which frame the Johannine passion speak to me particularly about the conquest of fear. The scene is set in the initial confrontation in the garden beyond the Kedron, where the powers of good and evil are ranged against each other, and the final battle beween light and darkness commences. Later, in the other garden across the city, it becomes clear that evil has been vanquished in the hour of Jesus. As Joseph and Nicodemus emerge from the night and the secrecy which have been their cover, it becomes evident that the revelation and action of love which constitute that hour have begun to dissipate the darkness.

Reflection on my own life experience and on what others have shared with me over the years has convinced me that fear is at the core of the power of darkness. Fear holds us back from surrendering to God. Perhaps it is the fear of losing ourselves, losing control; perhaps the fear of ultimately being found wanting. Fear renders trust impossible. Frequently fear prevents us from reaching out to others; it is an obstacle to intimacy and friendship, to community and collaboration, to service and self-giving. Fear stifles compassion. Fear thwarts growth, deadens dreams, cramps initiative, crushes potential, saps life-energy. So much of the aggression and violence within and around us is born of fear, and sustained and fuelled by it. Joseph and Nicodemus, and the disciples later in the upper room, barricaded behind closed doors (Jn 20:19), were held bound by fear.

Jesus once said:

> You will know the truth, and the truth will set you free (Jn 8:32).

And again:

> If then the Son sets you free, you will indeed be free (Jn 8:36).

I believe that this liberating truth is the realisation that God is love (1 Jn 4:8). God's love for us is revealed in that God sent the Son into the world that we might have life through him (1 Jn 4:9). 'In love there is no room for fear' (1 Jn 4:18). The two disciples, Joseph and Nicodemus, no longer walking in the dark, but in the light of life (Jn 8:12), free from fear, remind us of what is possible in our lives too, through the Spirit released in the hour, and beckon us to 'come to know and believe in the love which God has for us' (1 Jn 4:16).

THE GARDEN OF MEETING

The garden of burial, so near the place of death, becomes the garden of life. It is the scene of the encounter between the risen Jesus and Magdalen, a narrative which B. Rigaux once described as a little masterpiece from both the literary and theological viewpoints.[6]

The story so far

Our story begins 'early on the first day of the week, while it was still dark' (Jn 20:1). This detail, which contrasts

---

6 B. Rigaux, *Dio l'ha Risuscitato* (Milano, Edizioni Paolini 1976), p. 323. See also R.H. Fuller, *The Formation of the Resurrection Narratives* (London, SPCK 1972); C.F. Evans, *Resurrection and the New Testament* (London, SCM 1970; X. Leon-Dufour, *Resurrection and the Message of Easter* (London, Chapman 1974).

with the Synoptic 'at first light', probably has symbolic
significance for the fourth evangelist. It hints at the
darkness which engulfed Jesus' followers because of the
recent events, and their lack of readiness for what was
yet to take place. Mary of Magdala comes to the tomb.
In this version she comes alone, whereas in the Synoptics
she is accompanied, which would seem more likely. The
purpose of her visit is not specified. Since Jesus, as we
have seen, was lavishly anointed before burial, as befitted
a king (Jn 19:30-40), there would be no reason for her
to have that concern. In John's eyes, she probably comes
to the tomb with an aching heart to mourn her beloved
master.

On arriving, she observes that the stone has already
been moved away from the entrance; maybe she takes a
look inside, though this is not mentioned; and she rushes
off to tell Simon Peter and the beloved disciple:

> They have taken the Lord out of the tomb, and we do
> not know where they have laid him (Jn 20:2).

It is clear that Mary is not expecting a resurrection. She
interprets the tomb's emptiness in terms of theft, which
was not uncommon at the time, an act presumably perpe-
trated by Jesus' enemies or by ordinary tomb-robbers.

Peter and 'the other disciple' then come running to the
tomb. The latter reaches the tomb first, spurred on by
deeper love, and sees the linen cloths, but stands aside
in deference to Peter. On arriving, Peter rushes straight
inside, and observes the wrappings and neatly folded head
napkin. He confirms that the tomb is empty, and dispels
the suspicion of theft. His companion then enters also,
and he, the evangelist tells us, 'saw and believed' (Jn 20:8).
There is some discussion amongst scholars about the
nature of this belief. Some take it to denote full resurrection

faith. 'The faith of the Beloved Disciple, the founding father, the inspiration and the model disciple for this community, was rooted in his journey into a recognition that death could not hold Jesus of Nazareth (neither tomb nor cloths) and that once risen, unlike Lazarus who had to be unbound (see Jn 11:44), he was forever free of the reality of death.'[7] The empty tomb holds a message; the disciple has understood this message; it leads him to faith in the risen Jesus.

This view is reflected in some translations of the subsequent comment of the evangelist:

> Until then they had not understood the scriptures, which showed that he must rise from the dead (Jn 20:9; NJB is similar).

Others prefer to speak of incipient, and, as yet, imperfect faith. De la Potterie comments that the empty tomb, the linen cloths and rolled up napkin serve as a sign, leading the disciple to believe that he is face to face with a mysterious action of God.[8] But he does not fully understand. John's observation can also be rendered: 'for as yet they did not understand the scripture, that he must rise from the dead' (NRSV). The conclusion of the episode seems to corroborate this view: 'The disciples went home again (Jn 20:10). They are puzzled; any faith which they may have is at this stage embryonic and fragile.

Mary must have returned to the tomb with them, though this is not indicated explicitly. It is at this juncture that we take up the story.

---

7   F.J. Moloney, 'John 20: a Journey Completed' in *The Australasian Catholic Record*, vol. lix, no 4, 1982, p. 426. See also J.W. Pryor, *John*, p. 87.
8   I. de la Potterie, *The Hour*, pp. 201-207.

Magdalen and Jesus

The first aspect of this narrative, which I find particularly
and poignantly striking, is the extraordinary depth of
Magdalen's love for Jesus. When the men go away, she
remains, standing by the tomb, alone, unwilling to leave.
Her overwhelming grief at Jesus' death is intensified by
her distress at the disappearance of the body. She lingers
there, weeping and searching.

Then there is the subtle alteration between her response
now to the angels' question and the statement made earlier
to Simon and the beloved disciple. To the latter she said:

> They have taken the Lord out of the tomb, and we do
> not know where they have laid him (Jn 20:2).

To the two angels in white who now enquire as to the
reason for her tears, she replies:

> They have taken *my* Lord away, and *I* do not know where
> they have laid him (Jn 20:13).

The switch from plural to singular is significant. It brings
out her personal relationship with Jesus. The topic of
personal relationship recurs throughout the supper discourses, and it is also an important element in John's
understanding of the resurrection.

A key theme in the resurrection narratives, as indeed
throughout the fourth gospel, is the process of growth
in faith. At this stage in the story, Mary's tears show that
she has no idea that Jesus has been raised; she is convinced
that his body has been transported to another place. And,
as she rather impractically tells the 'gardener', she wants
to know where, so that she can take him away. There is
still a heavy emphasis on absence rather than presence.
At the same time, her words seem to betray a certain
possessiveness: she speaks of '*my* Lord', as though he is

hers alone. As well as growth in faith, the narrative is about an opening out, an expansion of love.

One of the features of all the resurrection narratives in the New Testament is the theme of non-recognition, hesitancy, doubt. Whilst this can serve an apologetic purpose, in that it illustrates that the disciples, and here Mary Magdalen, were in no way expecting a resurrection, its principal significance is theological. It shows that Jesus has undergone a change. It is a constituent of the continuity/transformation scheme, the sameness/difference model adopted for the kerygmatic presentation of the resurrection. So now the angels fade from the scene, and Jesus is standing there. From absence to presence – this is the next move of the narrative. Mary turns and sees him, but she fails to recognise him, even when he initiates the conversation with the question about the cause of her grief.

There is, I think, something deeply touching, almost desperate, about the way in which she rushes to seek from him a solution to her quest for the body:

> If it is you, sir, who removed him, tell me where you have laid him, and I will take him away (Jn 20:15).

She turns away and the 'gardener' calls her name: 'Mary!' She recognises that voice, unique in all the world. She turns to face him, an outward sign of inner openness, and cries: 'Rabbuni!' – 'My Master!' Here we encounter once more the beautiful Johannine theme of the good shepherd, who knows his sheep by name, and whose sheep recognise his voice. Perhaps there is also an echo of the words of Isaiah 43:1: 'I have called you by your name' (NJB). It is the shepherd going in search of his sheep, paradoxically when she is searching for him. The intensely joyful moment of recognition is profoundly personal.

Mary's deep affection is transparent in the tone of her 'Rabbuni', and in her throwing herself at him.

The implication, however, seems to be that Mary believes that Jesus has returned as he was before. The title is basically the old title used in the ministry; in John 1:38 it marks the *beginning* of the disciples' faith journey. Her holding or clinging, natural, beautiful and spontaneous as it is, denotes that the 'Jesus whom Mary sees is the Jesus of the past, Jesus before his death'.[9] Now that he has come back into her life, Mary does not want to let him go. She wants the former relationship to be resumed. She wishes to recapture the conditions of previous experience. There is a further stage of growth in faith and in love to be accomplished.

Jesus then seeks to lead her to Easter faith and to an entirely new dimension of relationship. He says to her:

> Do not cling to me, for I have not yet ascended to the Father (Jn 20:17).

I would like to link this injunction with the question which Jesus asked her on first approaching her in the garden. As well as the angelic enquiry: 'Why are you weeping?' he asks, very significantly: 'Whom are you looking for?' cf. Jn 18:4). Mary was then seeking an absent corpse. As elsewhere in the Gospel, the question suggests that she should be seeking not only for the living Jesus, 'Jesus of Nazareth', but for Jesus in the depths of his identity and mystery, the Jesus now glorified through his hour.

---

9   See I. de la Potterie, *The Hour*, p. 213. For his insightful treatment of the
     Magdalen episode, see pp. 207-215. I am also particularly indebted to R.E.
     Brown, *John*, pp. 980-1017.

At the supper Jesus said:

> You will look for me, and, as I told the Jews, I tell you
> now: where I am going you cannot come (Jn 13:33).

And in subsequent discourse:

> I came from the Father and have come into the world;
> and now I am leaving the world again and going to the
> Father (Jn 16:28).

Jesus, having come 'from above' (Jn 3:31), remains
throughout his life 'turned towards the bosom of the
Father' (Jn 1:18), bent on accomplishing his Father's will,
the task for which he was sent. The climax of that task
consists of his being lifted up, uplifted on the cross,
uplifted in resurrection/ascension. This upward movement
effects his return to his Father's house, thus constituting
his glorification. Then it is that he can send the Spirit,
the Paraclete, from the Father (Jn 15:26; 16:7).

It is instructive to recall those other very beautiful words
of Jesus at the supper which provide background for this
scene:

> Set your troubled hearts at rest. Trust in God always;
> trust also in me. There are many dwelling-places in my
> Father's house; if it were not so I should have told you;
> for I am going there on purpose to prepare a place for
> you. And if I go and prepare a place for you, I shall
> come again and take you to myself, so that where I am
> you may be also (Jn 14:1-3).

Jesus, then, is leading Mary away from the past into the
future; leading her from one type of presence, through
absence, to another form of presence; leading her to fuller
understanding of his identity as the only Son of the Father,
'full of grace and truth' (Jn 1:14); leading her to the insight
which constitutes Easter faith: 'I have seen the Lord!'

She comes to realise that Jesus has not come back to what
he was before. He is not *her* Lord, *her* Master. He has
become the risen Lord. Now she is able to loosen her
hold, to cease her clinging, to let him go. His returning
to the Father's side will make possible a new form of
presence, creating a new depth and dimension of relationship and intimacy through the gift of the Spirit, that
indwelling or making one's home in about which he spoke
at the supper. His return thus enables him to mediate
full companionship with God to them all, the fruit of
his completed work.[10]

Having led Mary to faith, Jesus next sends her to share
her understanding and her joy with the disciples, whom
he refers to affectionately as brothers (and presumably as
sisters too, since the Greek word means siblings of both
sexes):

> Go to my brothers and tell them that I am ascending
> to my Father and your Father, to my God and your God
> (Jn 20:17).

For some scholars, this beautifully balanced phrasing
emphasises both the otherness or separateness of Jesus,
and his closeness and belonging. For others, it is remin-
iscent of Ruth 1:16 ('Your God will be my God') and the
covenant formulas of Jeremiah 31:3, and Ezekiel 36:28
('I shall be their God and they shall be my people'). The
Father of Jesus has, through the Son's uplifting, become

---

10   See R. Schnackenburg, *St John*, vol 3, pp. 317-320; R.E. Brown comments
     that the statement 'I am ascending to my Father' is not a determination
     of the time and has no implications for the state of the risen Jesus previous
     to that statement. 'It is a theological statement contrasting the passing nature
     of Jesus' presence in his post-resurrectional appearances and the permanent
     nature of his presence in the Spirit', *John*, p. 1015.

their Father. Through faith in him, through begetting by the Spirit, they become children of God and the purpose of the Word's becoming flesh is achieved (Jn 1:12). The uplifted one draws all to himself (Jn 12:32), draws all into the mystery of the Father's enduring love. For the first time the disciples are referrd to as the brothers and sisters of Jesus. The new covenant people, the new family of God, comes into being. This message is, then, John's formulation of the kerygma, the Good News of salvation.

So Mary of Magdala retraces her steps to bring this news to the disciples. This time it is news, not about an empty tomb, but about a risen Lord. Her message is no longer a message of sadness and perplexity, but a joyful message of conviction and hope and promise:

I have seen the Lord! (Jn 20:18).

This seeing carries the full Johannine significance. She has come and seen (Jn 1:38). Jesus has revealed to her his glory (Jn 2:11). She has come to the faith that Jesus is the Christ, the Son of God. She can make her own the words of Jesus to Nicodemus: 'We speak of what we know, and testify to what we have seen' (Jn 3:11).

CONCLUSION

The Fourth Evangelist presents Mary of Magdala as a beloved disciple, no less than the disciple who reclined close to Jesus at the supper. Her love for him is profound. John also presents her as the first person to whom the risen Jesus appeared, and (probably) the first person to come to resurrection faith. In response to his injunction, she becomes the apostle to the apostles, the first to bear testimony to the exaltation of Jesus and its life-giving effects, the first to be commissioned to proclaim the kerygma.[11] The narrative portrays her faith journey, which is also her love journey. One feature of that twofold journey is the element of letting go.

In recent months I have been thinking a great deal about 'letting go'. My term of office as Salesian Provincial in the UK came to an end, and whilst there was much that I was delighted to relinquish, there were aspects of this ministry which I found fulfilling and enjoyable, and was sorry to lose. A number of friends and colleagues have also had to change jobs and roles, which sometimes entailed considerable geographical displacement. I have become very aware of many people obliged to come to terms with aspects of the letting go which come with ageing or sickness. Letting go is also a feature of friendship, and it is a crucial stage or element in the parent-child relationship, in education, and also in religious formation settings. At times we need to let go of our hurts no less than of our hopes. And there is the letting go involved in death.

So often we want people and places and situations to remain the same; we want to stave off the advent of night-fall, as it were. We wish to cling, to hold on grimly and tightly, especially to what is beautiful and good and life-giving; to what brings affirmation and security; to what may touch our identity profoundly; to what gives meaning. Yet, other dimensions, not even dreamed of, can emerge

---

11 S. Schneiders, 'Women in the Fourth Gospel and the Role of Women in the Contemporary Church', in *Biblical Theology Bulletin* 12 (1982), pp. 35-45, draws from this the conclusion that women are called by Jesus to full discipleship and ministry in the Christian community.

and blossom when our hands are open, our arms empty, and we have turned round, and begun to look elsewhere. Like Magdalen, we may experience that letting go can be liberating, and can lead to deeper love and fuller life. Whereas, we and others can be impoverished and diminished by our continuing to cling.

A motif which links our Jerusalem gardens and merits our reflection is suggested by the question which Jesus puts firstly to his enemies in the arresting party, and later to Magdalen: 'Whom are you looking for?' (Jn 18:4; 20:15). In the story, the question is asked and answered at different levels. It opens up a perspective on the meaning and quality of our discipleship, the depth of our trust and love. Who is the Jesus of our searching, and where in fact are we seeking him, and why? The happy paradox is that, in our searching, we are ourselves being sought by the one who calls us by name, frees us to walk in the light of life, invites us to dwell in his love, and sends us to share in his mission.

8 | VINES OF FRIENDSHIP

One of the most beautiful sights in many parts of Europe and south eastern Australia is a vineyard in the early morning sun, as it catches the light and hugs the hillside. The same was true of the Palestine of Jesus' day. It is only to be expected that, as well as enjoying the fruit of the vine, Jesus, who was so in touch with his environment, should have used this imagery in his teaching. In this he was following a familiar and fertile tradition in the religious history of his people.[1] References to vineyards and vines are frequent in the Synoptic parables (cf. Mk 12:1-9; Mt 20:1-6; 21:28-32; 21:33-41; Lk 13:6-9; 20:9-16), but it is the use of this imagery of John which I propose to choose as the topic for our consideration in this final chapter.

---

1   For a survey of the biblical background, see R.E. Brown, *John*, pp. 669-672. Again the reader is referred to the commentaries on John listed in chapter 2, note 1.

The Fourth Evangelist presents the metaphor of vine
and branches within the context of the Lord's Supper,
where he draws together in a sublime synthesis comprising
three or four separate discourses the message of Jesus for
his own. This section of the Gospel, consisting of chapters
13-17, has a lengthy and complex history. The repetitive
nature of the text can be disconcerting, and suggests the
eventual sewing together of several forms of the tradition,
continually reworked over many years, as the community
recalled, and retold, the story of Jesus.[2]

These discourses contain some of John's loftiest and
most perceptive reflections on the person, and role, and
mystery of the Son. They also provide some of his warmest
and most moving insights into Jesus' humanity. Taking
these five chapters in one wide sweep, I find so much
that is breathtaking and poignant, as Jesus, aware of his
impending return to the Father through the suffering of
his hour, shares his deepest thoughts and feelings with
those with whom he has been sharing his everyday life.
It is fascinating to observe the subtle shift of mood and
tone. We catch the pain of parting and separation, the
devastation of betrayal by a friend, the protective concern
for the future well-being of his disciples, the ache and
longing to remain with them, the strong desire to reassure
and, above all, the amazing richness of his affection. From
this enormous wealth of material, I would like to reflect
with you on three points: disclosure, intimacy and
fruitfulness.

2   See F.J. Moloney, 'A Sacramental Reading of John 13:1-38' in *The Catholic
     Biblical Quarterly*, vol 53, no 2 (1991), pp. 240-241. He suggests a very helpful
     structure in 'The Structure and Message of John 15.1-16.3' in *Australian
     Biblical Review*, vol 35 (1987), pp. 35-49. See also J.W. Pryor, *John*, pp. 54-72,
     and 102-106.

A WAY OF DISCIPLESHIP

At one point in the discourse Jesus says:

> I have disclosed to you everything that I heard from my Father (Jn 15:15).

Throughout this Gospel Jesus is presented as the revealer. He is the Word of God, the supreme communication and unique *self-disclosure* of God, enfleshed.

> No one has ever seen God; God's only Son, he who is nearest to the Father's heart, has made him known (Jn 1:18).

> I do not mean that anyone has seen the Father; he who has come from God has seen the Father, and he alone (Jn 6:46).

Much of John's rich imagery suggests this revelation motif. Jesus is the *light* of the world (Jn 9:5), a theme illustrated in the cleverly constructed drama of the cure of the man born blind. He is the source of *living* water, a claim developed in his encounter with the Samaritan woman (Jn 4:1-42). He is the *bread of life*, which in the earlier part of the famous discourse of chapter 6 is generally thought to refer primarily to revelation. Jesus knows the heart of God, the mind of God. He has been taught by the Father (Jn 8:28); the Father dwelling in him is the source of the words he speaks (Jn 14:10). His mission is to make the Father known, and at the conclusion of his final prayer, he can claim to have revealed to his own the Father's name, the very being of God (Jn 17:26). This he does by his teaching, his words, and by his action, the signs which he works; but he does so especially by who he is, and such disclosure is much more immediate.

> If you knew me, you would know my Father too... Anyone who has seen me has seen the Father (Jn 14:7-9).

There is no need for special visions or theophanies (cf. Ex 33:18), for, in disclosing himself to his disciples, Jesus is the window into the mystery of God.

Such self-disclosure is an expression of Jesus' love, as he affirms in John 14:21. It is also an invitation to *intimacy*, to friendship, to the one-ing and bonding of persons, to a shared existence like vine and branches.

> Father... I make your name known to them, and will make it known, so that the love you had for me may be in them, and I may be in them (Jn 17:26).

The theme of being in, remaining in, abiding, indwelling, is a key Johannine concept, and connotes being immersed in love, surrounded by love, with an assurance of permanence. It is the central idea of the first section of the vine allegory (Jn 15:1-11). Jesus is the true vine, and issues to the disciples the invitation:

> Dwell in me, as I in you (Jn 15:4a) – (or, as another translation puts it), Make your home in me as I make mine in you.

> As the Father has loved me, so I have loved you. Dwell in my love (Jn 15:9).

This love theme is taken up again in the next section (Jn 15:12-17):

> You are my friends... No longer do I call you servants, for a servant does not know what his master is about. I have called you friends, because I have disclosed to you everything that I heard from my Father (Jn 15:14-15).

The texture of his friendship is overwhelmingly rich, for it is rooted in the relationship which Jesus shares with the Father. It is a love to the uttermost (Jn 13:1), for there is nothing greater that can be done for one's friends than to give one's life for them (Jn 15:13; cf. 10:18). 'Life sacrificed in death is the supreme gift, and the mark of love'.[3] And it is the knowledge stemming from self-disclosure which distinguishes a friend from a slave.

The friendship of Jesus includes a strong dimension of concern and solicitude, and the firm assurance that 'the Father loves you' (Jn 16:27):

> Set your troubled hearts at rest, and banish your fears (Jn 14:27).

> Trust in God always; trust also in me. There are many dwelling-places in my Father's house; if it were not so I should have told you; for I am going there to prepare a place for you. And if I go and prepare a place for you, I shall come again and take you to myself, so that where I am, you may be also... (Jn 14:1-3).

> Father, I do not pray you to take them out of the world, but to keep them from the evil one... Father, they are your gift to me; and my desire is that they may be with me where I am (Jn 17:15,24).

Jesus' words of love flow out, wave after wave, drawing us into the sea of his intimacy.

In the context of the imagery of the vine and branches, this intimacy and friendship, this abiding and mutuality, are intrinsically linked with *fruitfulness*. The vinedresser cuts away the fruitless or dead branch, and prunes the fruitful branch to make it bear even more (Jn 15:2). And,

> No branch can bear fruit by itself, but only if it remains united with the vine; no more can you bear fruit, unless you remain united with me (Jn 15:40).

> Anyone who dwells in me, as I dwell in him, bears much fruit; apart from me you can do nothing (Jn 15:5).

---

3   C.K. Barrett, *John*, p.477.

> This is how my Father is glorified: you are to bear fruit
> in plenty and so be my disciples (Jn 15:8).

The total dependency of branch on vine could be not more forcefully stated. Everything hinges on the disciple's incorporation in Jesus. Life and empowerment are drawn from the vine. The fruitfulness which the evangelist is speaking of at this point does not seem to be understood mainly in terms of missionary outreach. The love which Jesus has for us is a love which leads to our personal growth and development – to our having life in all its fullness. Our mutual abiding leads to deeper love, as love responds to love, and we are caught up in the meaning of his life and being. Abiding includes the element of ongoing commitment. This love finds its natural expression in obedience, according to the pattern of Jesus' loving surrender to the Father's will. 'The fruit of being a disciple of Jesus grows in the soil of love, as a gift of Jesus' love, and is essentially love itself, as Jesus demonstrated it'.[4]

The relationship of intimacy and the disciple's response of obedience lead to a reaching out to share life and love with others. Jesus' commandment is that we love one another, and the pattern and model of such servant loving is his own love for us (Jn 15:12; 13:15; 13:34-35). It is a love prepared to wash feet and to give self in death.

Several times during the supper discourses we are reminded that the Father is glorified in the Son (Jn 13:31; 14:13; 17:4), through his obedience and the fulfilment of his task, that for which he came into the world. Now Jesus extends that; the Father is glorified through the fruitfulness of those who are at one with the Son, through their obedience, shown in the quality of their mutual love.

Finally, in language which has a more formal and official ring, which perhaps hints at wider missionary outreach, Jesus tells his disciples:

> You did not choose me,
> no, I chose you;
> I commissioned you to go out and to bear fruit,
> fruit that will last (Jn 15:16 NJB).

This verse, in fact, fulfils a climactic and pivotal role. For, in stating: 'You did not choose me: I chose you', Jesus emphasises the giftedness of his disclosure, of his intimacy, and of ensuing fruitfulness and sharing of mission. God has gratuitously taken the initiative in sending the Son as the light of the world, as the self-disclosure of God, and as the source of eternal life, the communicator of the life of God. The Son has freely chosen the disciples to be recipients of this revelation and sharers in this life, has drawn them into an abiding relationship of love, into a community of love, and into the sharing of his mission. He refers to his choosing his disciples also in John 6:70 and 13:18; and they are sent out to the nations in John 20:21 after the giving of the Spirit: 'as the Father sent me, so I send you'. Mission flows from mutality, from indwelling, and the fruitfulness of mission springs from the quality of our love for Jesus which flows outward in self-giving service. As disciples, it is our love which bears witness to our relationship with Jesus, and is a reflection of Jesus' love for us, and of the mutual love which exists eternally between the Father and the Son.[5] Such love

5   See C.K. Barrett, *John*, p.476

continues to be revelation and source of life. All this takes place in an economy of gift.

In the triadic pattern of disclosure-intimacy-fruitfulness, John offers us a paradigm of Christian existence, Christian aliveness, this dynamic gift of our abiding in Christ Jesus. The elements ebb and flow in an ongoing movement of life and growth; they overlap in the cyclic interplay between contemplation and action. This pattern can, I believe, also shed some light on our relationships and on our prayer.

A MODEL FOR RELATIONSHIPS

One of our fundamental human drives and needs moves us in the direction of relating to others, to connectedness and, more deeply, in the direction of friendship, interpersonal intimacy. That this is so comes as no surprise, if we are indeed fashioned in God's image, and if, to use St Aelred of Rievaulx' rendering of 1 John 4:8,16: 'God is friendship ... and those who dwell in friendship are dwelling in God, and God in them'.[6]

To reach human and Christian fulfilment we need to be able to establish and sustain real friendships. We are made for, and called to, friendship. It was St Thomas Aquinas who wrote that the highest form of love is friendship.[7] Friendship is the most beautiful of all human experiences, an experience which can break us open so

6   Aelred of Rievaulx, (A. Squire, ed.) *Spiritual Friendship* (Kalamazoo, Cistercian Publications 1977), p.66.
7   See his Comment. on Sentences I, d.27, q.2a, 1-4. The text can be found in Mary T. Clark (ed), *An Aquinas Reader* (London, Hodder & Stoughton 1974), p.267.

that we can know God. One of the most penetrating descriptions of friendship is, I believe, that contained in the passage which we have been considering: 'Dwell in me as I dwell in you' or 'Make your home in me as I make mine in you', a union of mind and heart and being, in which unique individuality and profound interrelatedness coalesce and enhance each other.

An integral part of the development of human relationships and friendship and mutuality is *self-disclosure*. This is an ongoing process, 'whereby we freely share information about ourselves in a personal way'.[8] We can, it is true, get to know quite a lot about a person through observation, sensitive listening, and intuition. Here I am referring to the unfolding of our story from the inside, the revealing of aspects of ourselves and our experience, our mystery, which are normally hidden, often very private, always sacred.

Such disclosure presupposes a certain level of self-awareness; a lack of such awareness is one of the main barriers to communication. Disclosure consists in a sharing of ideas, aspirations, hopes and dreams, or anxieties, fears, struggles and problems; a confiding of feelings and experiences, our disappointments, perhaps, and disillusionment, our failures and brokenness, our joys, and vision, and faith. It demands a willingness to trust, to entrust oneself to the other; a willingness to become vulnerable, to dismantle some of our defences, to acknowledge in the hearing of another what is inside. One of the deepest needs of the human heart is to be understood, accepted and

8   R. Hammett and L. Sofield, *Inside Christian Community* (Dublin, Gill & Macmillan 1984), p. 81.

loved. 'We will only be known and loved as we really are, insofar as we are willing to reveal our true selves to others. We can only do this to the extent that we are in touch with the deeper things in our hearts.'[9]

If such disclosure is received with what Henri Nouwen calls 'hospitality'[10] and Evelyn Woodward 'empathy',[11] with respectful attention and non-judgmental acceptance, appreciation, warmth and understanding, the relationship tends to grow. Often reciprocal disclosure is called forth, at least later; friendship and interpersonal *intimacy* develop. On the other hand, criticism, moralising, or rejection, when one has been prepared to share, can be devastatingly hurtful and destructive. Such responses reinforce mistrust, low self-esteem, fear and defensiveness, which are the greatest obstacles to disclosure and growth, and which lock relationships in cramping ordinariness and superficiality.

Genuine friendships are *fruitful* and lifegiving. The acceptance and affirmation of another enable self-acceptance, give a sense of worth, an at-homeness and peace with oneself, the realisation that it is good to be me, a feeling of well-being. I become more self-aware and more integrated. Awareness that I am known, understood, accepted and loved is liberating. It bestows confidence and assurance, and releases creativity. Where friendship is lacking, we find apathy, flatness, deadness, boredom, isolation, cynicism. Friendship brings meaning and alive-

---

9 P. Collins, *Intimacy and the Hungers of the Heart* (Dublin, Columba 1991), p. 111. My original draft of the second and third parts of this chapter has been confirmed and enriched by my recent acquaintance with this book.
10 H. Nouwen, *Reaching Out* (London, Collins 1976), pp. 61-101.
11 E. Woodward, *Poets, Prophets and Pragmatists* (Melbourne, Collins Dove 1987), p. 55.

ness, zest and purposefulness. It actualises so much potential latent within. Gifts and capabilities blossom. Qualities of kindness and compassion and generosity grow, as we are freed and empowered to reach out and genuinely serve others. Our lives become so much more fruitful and life-giving. For love of its nature spills out and soaks all around, like mountain water bursting over the edge of a wayside trough.

I believe that this pattern can also shed light on the dynamic of growth of any Christian group, whether that be a religious community, a prayer group, or a team in ministry in a wide range of settings. Admittedly, the parallel is not exact; friendship and what may be termed professional mutuality do not always coincide; the purpose and focus of the particular group must always be borne in mind. However, I still believe that this dynamic is illuminating and challenging.

In any of these group settings, we come together in order to live out more authentically our Christian discipleship. Wherever we are, and whatever we are engaged in, an essential aspect of our response to the gospel is the overcoming of division and the creating of communion; and another essential is mission, through witness and apostolic outreach. The Johannine image of vine and branches, the new commandment of love, his presentation of Jesus' mission in terms of drawing all to himself (Jn 12:32) and gathering into one the scattered children of God (Jn 11:52), and the prayer that his followers might be one (Jn 17:21), merge to form an inescapable and cogent challenge. Even if we understand the purpose of our coming together as primarily task oriented, rather than supportive, we cannot afford to underestimate the importance of the quality of relationships within the group, the level of genuine mutuality achieved.

We are called to develop mutuality because it is central
to our Christian vision. Obviously, there are degrees of
closeness in our relating. We are called to work at
mutuality also, because of the nature of our mission, which
is to witness to the possibility, the reality of a love and
unity beyond, and through, distinctions and differences.
We are also called to strive towards mutuality because
the quality of relationships in the group or community
can, through the affirmation, trust and challenge
engendered, make us more effective, more fruitful in
minstry.

Such growth in mutuality leading to fruitfulness
demands some self-disclosure, a 'willingness to share
appropriate parts of one's story and to listen with empathy
to the stories of others'.[12] Such disclosure can, of course,
be costly and demanding. It is necessary to discern what
level and kind of disclosure is appropriate for the type
of group, and for the particular situation. One must be
sensitive to others' needs, and feelings, and expectations.
Respect for confidentiality is required, and for people's
privacy and personal space. Reluctance and fear and
unease will have to be overcome gradually.

But when we can share something of our values and
vision and dreams together, and also our struggles and
problems in our Christian response, it is my experience
that the group becomes more alive as a Christian group.
Horizons broaden, vision is clarified and sharpened, gifts
and expertise surface and can be harnessed; we can find
greater strength in facing challenges and problems;
commitment is firmed up. Above all, trust is developed.

---

12 See E. Woodward, *Poets, Prophets and Pragmatists*, p. 52. In this section
I have drawn on her reflections on pages 36-64.

We are enriched and empowered. Our life and work and witness are more fruitful.

I am reminded of a haunting phrase in the little book entitled *Hope for the Flowers*[13] which suggests that many caterpillars die without ever knowing that they were meant to become butterflies. It could serve as an epitaph of many religious groupings within the Church. For we can settle for safe and effortless mediocrity, remain gnarled and withered branches, producing the odd grape or two maybe, but nothing like the joy-filled abundance of Cana! The symbol of vine and branches offers us a pattern of ministry.

A PARADIGM OF PRAYER

Prayer has been described as 'being yourself before God'.[14] Just as in human relationships real genuineness (truth) demands that I am me – no role playing, no pretending that I am what I am not, or I am not what I am – so also in prayer it is essential that I am me when I encounter God. I come into the Lord's presence simply as me. God is very comfortable with that. I suspect, however, that many of us have problems in prayer because we are not comfortable with ourselves. We are not at home with ourselves; we are not convinced that it is good to be me; we have not yet really accepted ourselves. Perhaps we are not comfortable with God either! The deep-down image which we have of God can be alarmingly different from the loving, forgiving, compassionate God of Jesus,

---

13 cf. Trina Paulus, *Hope for the Flowers* (Newman-Smith, Richardson, Texas 1972).
14 T.N. Hart, *The Art of Christian Listening* (New York, Paulist 1980), p. 52.

whose mercy, as Tournier puts it, is boundless and unmerited, whose love is unconditional and all-inclusive, whose acceptance and approval utterly unreserved.[15] Beneath the surface, often unknown to us, there can be lurking an image of a harsh, demanding, punitive God inspiring fear, resentment, anxiety. Inevitably, this has an adverse effect on our praying. For, 'the extent to which a person feels loved by the Lord, is the extent that he or she will have both the inclination and the ability to pray'.[16]

As I come into God's presence, it is important to be aware of myself, of how I am feeling, of what is going on inside and around me. If I am weary, I am weary; if I am angry or frustrated, then I am angry or frustrated – there is no point in denying it! If I am hurting, I am hurting; if I am bursting with joy and excitement, that is how I am. It is amazing what bubbles gently to the surface, or rushes up violently, when once I fall still!

It is important to be in touch with these feelings (especially the feelings which I believe I should not have!), and with what lies behind them. This is me just now, and I disclose it to the Lord, simply and honestly. I can be sure of God's hospitality, God's welcome. 'Come as you are, that's how I love you', as one song puts it

It is also important to be aware of our desires, our deepest yearnings, and to articulate what it is for which I thirst, to reply to the question frequently on Jesus' lips: 'What do you want me to do for you?' (Mk 10:51) or 'What

---

15 P. Tournier, *Guilt and Grace* (London, Hodder & Stoughton 1962), p. 189. For further reflections on our image of God, see M.T. Winstanley, *Come and See*, pp. 1-14.
16 P. Collins, *Intimacy*, p. 190.

are you looking for?' (Jn 1:38). The Spirit is present in these longings. We listen to the Lord's response to our confiding.

Disclosure, however, is a two-way process, and prayer is the gift of God's self-disclosure to us. Such disclosure takes many forms. God speaks to me very strongly through nature. A few years ago I spent a marvellous week in the Val d'Aosta in the Italian Alps, courtesy of one of our Salesian communities. It is a place of breathtaking beauty, overlooked by the snowcapped Monte Rosa. Three lingering images of God's closeness and love are impressed upon my mind. There was the sense of being enfolded in mountains, strongly and securely, so that nothing could break in and wrench me away from that embrace. There was the endless supply of water, cascading with great force from melting glaciers, life-giving torrents, swirling and falling, engulfing me in a floodtide of love and unlimited forgiveness. And thirdly, there were the alpine flowers, a bewildering variety and shape and colour, exquisitely fashioned, growing in the most remote and unexpected places. It was as if God was saying: 'I am always around and I can always surprise you!' In such experiences I know that I am at one with my world, with its sounds and smells and sights and feel, and with the ground of all being and becoming.

God's disclosure comes also through other people. Frequently, I have recognised that presence in the clear, peace-filled eyes of the elderly; or in the excited wonder of a discovering child; or in the pain and helplessness of the sick; or in the love of a friend. I believe that the love of friendship is the most powerful imaging, mirroring, revealing of God's love, for in the look and touch and warmth of friendship, our personal worth is affirmed.

One very privileged place of encounter with God is
scripture. We call it God's word. It is not a dead word
from an alien culture and a distant past. For God is a
living God; God's word transcends boundaries of space
and time and culture. God's *self-disclosure* through the word
is a revelation and communication of who God is, what
God is like all the time, and an indication of what God
is doing and offering us everywhere and always.

Scripture presents us with a plethora of names which
we can use to address God. It provides many images and
metaphors which can convey something of God's distinc-
tive style of loving. It furnishes many narratives which
describe God's ways of saving. In the course of this book
we have considered many of these.

For instance, the name of shepherd, and the imagery
and narrative associated with it, can serve as a window
into the redeeming mystery of God, and as a key to understanding the ministry, death and resurrection of Jesus.
We are invited to adopt in prayer a stance which the
symbol calls for. Using our imagination, we can enter
into one of the shepherding scenes referred to earlier,
identifying with the lost sheep, or Magdalen, or Peter,
or the harassed crowd, feeling with them, or listening to
Jesus' words as addressed to us. Alternatively, we can take
one or several of the descriptive phrases employed by
Ezekiel or the psalmist or John, repeat them slowly, stay
with them, and allow them to speak to our heart. God
knows me and calls me by name in my uniqueness. The
Lord Jesus searches me out in my lostness, revives me
in my weariness and depression, heals me in my brokenness, carries me in his arms; I belong to him. He will
not allow me to perish. He calls me into the circle, the
fold of his love, that I may dwell in him, sharing his life

through the gift of the Spirit. In this way we can, I believe, come to a deeper appreciation of God's love, a more profound perception of the mystery which embraces us. We can come to *know* the Lord as our shepherd.

Or we can use the symbol of table companionship, and live the experience of sharing a meal with Jesus, like Levi, or the woman in Simon's house, or with Zacchaeus, or the disciples. Acknowledging our fragility and sinfulness, we can allow his acceptance and forgiveness to enfold us and permeate our being. Or we can identify with one or other of the little people, and come to Jesus in our poverty and need, and experience his words and actions of compassion. We can stand on Calvary and listen to the words of the dying Jesus, or gaze at his opened side, and allow the truth of his saving love to soak into us. Gradually, we come to know Jesus and the God whom he reveals.

Disclosure leads to *intimacy*. In such listening prayer we shall probably find that appropriate affections, feelings and sentiments will arise – gratitude, sorrow, trust, loyalty, joyful wonder, love, obedient surrender. As we respond, a dialogue of love will ensue. We shall gradually be drawn more completely into the relationship we share. We shall dwell in God and God in us, and we shall rest in God's love.

Such prayer, I believe, leads to *fruitfulness*, and does so in two ways. Firstly, it is in such communion that the Spirit transforms our hearts, fashioning and shaping them after the pattern of the heart of Jesus (the shepherd, the servant, the table companion, the compassionate healer, the accompanying friend...). Our attitudes, dispositions, values, outlook become more like his. We are slowly changed from within. We are drawn to make our own his lifestyle of surrender and self-giving service. Secondly, in coming to know more closely God's love for us and for all our sisters and brothers, we are moved and motivated to respond, to reach out to love and serve others as we are loved and served by God.[17]

> As I have loved you, so you are to love one another (Jn 13:34).

Drawn more fully by the Spirit into the relationship between the Father and the Son, the deepest longings of our heart will be fulfilled, as Jesus promised:

> Ask what you will, and you shall have it (Jn 15:7; cf. 15:16).

---

17 See W.C. Spohn, *What are they saying about Scriptures and Ethics?* (New York, Paulist 1984), pp. 106-128.

CONCLUSION

In the course of this book we have reflected on many scriptural passages and themes, and have spent time with Jesus in a variety of situations and settings. In the journey which we have made together many facets of God's love have been illustrated, as God seeks us out through Jesus.

We have seen with particular clarity God's compassion, providential presence, acceptance, and saving love. In the cadence of Jesus' voice, the warmth of his gaze, the touch of his hand, we have encountered the love of God enfleshed. Jesus, we believe, is 'the revelation, the laying bare of the very heart and being of ultimate reality'.[1] God is supremely gracious, and loves us with an everlasting love (Jer 31:3).

Together we have shared the experience of many people whose lives Jesus touched, and have been drawn into their

1   J.A.T.Robinson, *Honest to God* (London, SCM 1963), p. 128.

response of trust: the Magi and the little people; his Mother and those who shared his table; Magdalen and his disciples. It is my hope that we shall be able to pray more easily and with greater conviction and surrender the words which Luke places on the lips of the dying Jesus:

Father, into your hands I commit my spirit' (Jn 23:46).

This prayer of the evening of life is the Church's prayer for the evening of the day. Before we retire for the night we commit into God's hands the day which is coming to a close: the things which we have tried to do for the kingdom; the love we have received and given; the mistakes we have made; the opportunities grasped or missed; the difficulties which have arisen; the problems still unsolved; the anxieties which trouble us; the graced/gifted situations which we have recognised... And our prayer can stretch back far beyond this day to earlier stages of our journey, for often we fail to entrust our past into the Father's hands.

At all times there are people and situations that we may wish to commend to God's faithful care: people whom we love; those whom we seek to serve; people with whom we share life and ministry; in sickness and separation, in journeying, and struggle, and hope, and change. We know that the hands into which we commit them are gracious hands.

And finally, we can commit into God's hands our future, our personal future, especially in times of uncertainty, and the future of our families and communities, our Church and world, in the face of the problems and challenges which confront us. Aware of our anxieties and fears, and of our tendency to cling, we turn to the God of faithfulness and life, who is worthy of our total trust.

This prayer takes us right to the centre of the heart of Jesus. We are one with him in his loving and trusting surrender:

Into your hands ...

Biblical Studies Series